WITHDRAWN

100 Great Tapas

100 Great Tapas
Pippa Cuthbert

Photographs by Gareth Sambidge

CASSELL
ILLUSTRATED

First published in Great Britain in 2007 by Cassell Illustrated,
A division of Octopus Publishing Group Limited,
2–4 Heron Quays, London E14 4JP

A CIP catalogue record for this book is available from the
British Library.

ISBN-10: 1 84403 533 6
ISBN-13: 978 1 844035 33 5

Edited by Barbara Dixon
Design by Ashley Western
Photography by Gareth Sambidge
Prop Styling by Harriet Docker
Publishing Manager Anna Cheifetz

Printed in China

Contents

Introduction – The Tapa Experience

It's a balmy evening and I drag myself away from the Spanish sunshine and wafting smell of orange blossom to enter the cool interior of a bodega or wine bar. Multi-coloured tiles line the walls, barrels of wine and sherry are stacked in the corner and whole cured hams hang from the ceiling. But what is really drawing me in are the aromas of plate after plate of food being placed on the bar.

These small plates of food are 'tapas' and are the best introduction to the Spanish way of life. And what I love so much about tapas is that they are just that – a way of life, not just a way of eating. Although they are thought to have originated in the Andalusian city of Seville, tapas have become a huge focus of every Spaniard's life. At the end of a working day, locals will head to bars for their evening ritual of eating, drinking and chatting with friends – a ritual that since the 1980s has become popular all over the world. It is really a civilised way of drinking in which people move between bars, socialising and catching up on the day's news, watching soccer and relaxing. It is customary to stand up at the bar to sample the tapas with a small glass of beer, wine, or sherry. Tapas bars serve as de facto living rooms since entertaining at home, outside of the family, is uncommon in Spain. In the local tapas bar everyone mixes, regardless of social and economic status. This moveable feast from one bar to another is known as the 'Tapeo' and dinner is finally eaten sometime after 9.00pm or even later in the warmer months of summer.

There are many myths as to the origin of tapas and how this way of eating came to be such a part of the Spanish culture. Some believe it was enforced by the Spanish King Alfonso X, who insisted, in an attempt to keep stagecoach drivers sober, that all inns provided food when serving wine. It seems, however, that the most popular myth is that establishments would place a slice of cured ham, cheese, or bread over a glass of wine when it was served to prevent insects from falling in. Whatever the real story, tapas have become an iconic symbol of the Spanish culture.

The criteria for the success of a tapas dish is ultimately that it tastes good. True traditional Spanish food is based on raw, simple ingredients and has its roots firmly in home and country cooking. The style is robust and unpretentious and appearance is secondary. Ingredients are inexpensive, reflecting seasonality; and regional and traditional diversity is still evident. This simplistic yet indulgent way of eating little plates of food one after the other, just to tide you over to the next meal, has huge appeal to many people. The hardest part is to not let yourself eat too many. My recipes aim to encompass the real spirit of Spain while adding a contemporary dimension. Basically any dish can become a tapas as long as it is served in small portions and, consequently, any of my tapas recipes can become a main meal.

There are a number of ingredients and flavours that distinguish Spanish food. If you have ever driven through the Andalusian countryside where olive trees line the horizon in every direction, or smelt the strong aromas of orange blossom in Seville or Valencia you will know what I mean. In Catalonia rice fields provide the basis for the authentic dish Paella Valenciana and

the regions of Galicia and Asturias are renowned for their quality fish and shellfish. And while sometimes forgotten, the central plains of Spain produce the well-known Manchego cheese as well as numerous other sheep's cheeses. It is important also to remember the Moorish influences and their presence on the Iberian Peninsula as far back as the 7th century. The Moors brought with them exotic ingredients such as saffron, almonds and peppers, which are typical of Spanish cuisine today. Spain is a vast country that stretches north–south from France to Africa, and east–west from the Mediterranean to the Atlantic. What unites the Spanish is their inclination to eat well, drink wisely and ultimately enjoy life.

Spain has not only made a mark in the international culinary world for the excitement and variety that tapas can bring to our dining repertoire, but the likes of restaurants such as El Bulli, near Barcelona, and Arzak, at San Sebastian, have raised standards to another level. Their experimental cuisine, in which the science of food makes people stop and think, is opening up new doors for tapas. You will find my recipes cover everything you would hope to find in a tapas book, while adding new ideas to broaden our minds. While nowhere near as wacky and experimental as the food found at El Bulli, it's a chance for tapas to evolve. Most can be made quickly and easily, many can be made in advance and served at room temperature, while others can be partly prepared and finished off at the last minute. Basically any dish can become a tapas, so be imaginative and let the 'Tapeo' begin at home... Salud!

Olives, Dips & Breads

Andalusia is the land of olives. You may think it is sacrilege to fry olives — I did at first and am still not sure I'm convinced! But sometimes, when they are in such abundance, it makes a nice change.

Andalusian Fried Olives

100 g/3½ oz plain flour, for coating

1 egg, beaten

100 g/3½ oz dried breadcrumbs

500 g/1 lb 2 oz large stuffed green olives, of your choice

750 ml–1 litre/ 1¼–1¾ pints vegetable or sunflower oil

Serves 4–6 as part of a selection of tapas

Put the flour, egg and breadcrumbs in three separate bowls and line them up in order. Coat the olives in the flour, dip them into the beaten egg, then coat in the breadcrumbs. Set aside on a plate while you heat the oil.

Put the vegetable or sunflower oil in a large, heavy-based saucepan and heat to 190°C/375°F, or until a small cube of bread turns golden in about 30 seconds.

Fry the olives in the oil for 1–2 minutes, or until golden brown.

Using a slotted spoon, transfer to a plate and serve hot with a glass of chilled sherry.

Salted almonds are great as a tapa or just as a pre-dinner nibble with drinks. They can be made in advance and stored in a jar or airtight container until needed. Experiment with different flavours – chilli or cayenne pepper works well, as does ground cumin or coriander.

For true authenticity, seek out Marcona almonds if you can. These famously round almonds are from the Valencia and Alicante regions of Spain and have a rich, buttery, sweet flavour and a creamy texture.

Lemon Salted Almonds

15 g/½ oz butter

300 g/11 oz blanched almonds

1 tablespoon sea salt

1 tablespoon freshly ground black pepper

zest of 1 lemon

Makes 300 g/11 oz

Melt the butter in a large, non-stick frying pan and add the almonds. Fry over a medium heat for 6–8 minutes, stirring continuously, until they are golden brown.

Turn off the heat and stir in the salt, black pepper and lemon zest. Mix well, then arrange in a single layer on a large plate or tray lined with kitchen paper and leave to cool.

Store in an airtight jar until needed.

Salt and Fennel-Spiced Almonds

1 teaspoon fennel seeds

1 tablespoon sea salt flakes

½ teaspoon Spanish hot smoked paprika

15 g/½ oz unsalted butter

300 g/11 oz blanched almonds (preferably Marcona)

1 tablespoon dry Madeira

Makes 300 g/11 oz

(Illustrated overleaf)

Heat a dry, heavy-based saucepan or wok over a medium heat. Add the fennel seeds and salt and cook, stirring constantly, for about 3 minutes, or until the fennel seeds are lightly golden and aromatic. Transfer to a mortar and, using a pestle, grind to a fine powder. Stir in the paprika and set aside.

Melt the butter in the same pan and add the almonds. Fry over a medium heat for 6–8 minutes, stirring continuously, until they are golden brown.

Turn off the heat and stir in the Madeira, then add the fennel mixture. Mix well, then arrange in a single layer on a large plate or tray lined with kitchen paper and leave to cool.

Store in an airtight jar until needed.

Marinated olives are a deliciously simple tapa, which can be stored in the fridge for any unexpected guests. Using the basic formula below, try experimenting with different flavour combinations.

Marinated Olives

*Each makes
300 g/11 oz*

Fennel and Rosemary

300 g/11 oz green or black olives in brine, or a mixture

1 tablespoon white wine vinegar

50 ml/2 fl oz extra virgin olive oil

1 garlic clove, peeled and sliced

1 tablespoon fennel seeds

3 sprigs fresh rosemary

Coriander and Lemon

300 g/11 oz green or black olives in brine, or a mixture

1 tablespoon white wine vinegar

50 ml/2 fl oz extra virgin olive oil

1 tablespoon coriander seeds

zest of 1 lemon, cut into long shreds using a potato peeler

Chilli and Thyme

300 g/11 oz green or black olives in brine, or a mixture

1 tablespoon white wine vinegar

50 ml/2 fl oz extra virgin olive oil

½–1 teaspoon crushed chilli flakes

3 sprigs fresh thyme

Drain the olives from the brine and rinse briefly under running cold water. Using a small knife, make a slit down the side of each olive right down to the stone.

Combine the vinegar, olive oil and flavourings in a jug, then pour over the olives and mix well to coat.

Transfer the olives to an airtight container or jar and leave to marinate for at least 2 days for the flavour to develop, or for up to 3 months.

As well as being an addition to your cheese board, this recipe is great with grilled meats. I like to add it to a steak sandwich with plenty of garlic mayo or alioli, but to meet the tapas repertoire I've kept it small – simply spread on crostini with a slice of goat's cheese.

Caramelised Fennel and Onion Crostini with Goat's Cheese

1 tablespoon extra virgin olive oil

1 onion, peeled and thinly sliced

1 large fennel bulb, very thinly sliced

1 garlic clove, peeled and crushed

4 tablespoons caster sugar

1 tablespoon wholegrain mustard

2 tablespoons white cider or sherry vinegar

Crostini (see page 23)

50 g/2 oz goat's cheese, thinly sliced

salt and freshly ground black pepper

Makes 24–30

Heat the olive oil over a medium heat in a non-stick saucepan and add the onion, fennel and garlic. Stir until well coated in the oil and the onion and fennel start to soften but not brown. Increase the heat, add the sugar and stir constantly for a further 2–3 minutes, or until starting to brown.

Stir in the mustard and vinegar and season generously with salt and black pepper. When the liquid has evaporated, reduce the heat slightly and leave the mixture to caramelise and darken around the edges, stirring occasionally, for a further 8–12 minutes. Leave to cool.

Serve the fennel and onion mixture on prepared crostini and top with a slice of goat's cheese and a grind of black pepper.

Spread this over toasted breads, or use it to stuff cherry tomatoes. A spoonful can also be added to stews and casseroles as additional seasoning. It is an extremely versatile and delicious paste to keep a good stock of in the fridge.

This is a classic sauce from Catalonia, which traditionally contains romesco peppers and is often served with fish. In Tarragona, where it originates, it is made with both almonds and hazelnuts, but there are many versions today and mine is a slightly simplified one.

Black Olive Paste

Romesco Sauce

100 g/3½ oz
pitted black olives

1 tablespoon
capers, rinsed

6 tinned anchovy
fillets in oil, drained

15 g/½ oz fresh
flat-leafed parsley

2 tablespoons extra
virgin olive oil

freshly ground
black pepper

Makes about
150 g/5 oz

Put all the ingredients into the bowl of a food processor and whiz to a smooth paste.

Transfer to a bowl, cover with clingfilm and refrigerate until ready to serve. This will keep for up to 1 month.

50 ml/2 fl oz plus
2 tablespoons extra
virgin olive oil

100 g/3½ oz
blanched almonds

2 thick slices of white
bread, crusts removed

2 roasted
red peppers
(see page 134),
peeled and deseeded

2 garlic cloves,
peeled and
finely chopped

¼–½ teaspoon dried
chilli flakes

2 teaspoons sherry
vinegar or
cider vinegar

salt and freshly
ground black pepper

Makes about
250 ml/8 fl oz

(Illustrated overleaf)

Heat the 2 tablespoons of olive oil in a large, non-stick frying pan. Add the almonds and cook, stirring, for 4–6 minutes, or until golden brown. Remove the nuts and drain on kitchen paper.

Put the bread in the pan and fry on both sides until golden. Remove from the pan and put in a food processor with the almonds, peppers, garlic, chilli flakes, vinegar and remaining oil. Blend to a paste and season to taste.

Chill in the fridge for up to 2 weeks.

It's hard to beat a plain bread stick with a cold beer.
They're satisfying to make and even more satisfying to eat.

Bread Sticks

350 ml/12 fl oz tepid water

7 g/¼ oz sachet dried yeast, or 15 g/½ oz fresh yeast

500 g/1 lb 2 oz strong white bread flour, sifted, plus extra for dusting

1 teaspoon salt

2 teaspoons extra virgin olive oil, plus extra for greasing

2 teaspoon fine semolina

To flavour

choice of sea salt, sesame seeds, poppy seeds, rosemary, black pepper

Makes about 36

Pour 100 ml/3½ fl oz of the tepid water into a small bowl. Sprinkle on the yeast and leave for 5–10 minutes, then stir to dissolve.

Mix the flour and salt in a large bowl and make a well in the centre. Pour in the olive oil and yeasted water. Using a wooden spoon, draw the flour in from the sides, adding the remaining water as needed to form a firm but sticky dough.

Turn the dough out on to a lightly floured work surface and knead until it is smooth and elastic – about 10 minutes. Cover the dough with a tea towel and leave to rest for about 10 minutes. Knead the dough for a further 10 minutes.

Preheat the oven to 200°C/400°F/mark 6. Tear a small amount of dough (about 25 g/1 oz) from the ball at a time and, using the palm of your hand, roll to form a long, skinny, finger-like shape, about 25 cm/ 10 inches long. You can experiment with other shapes and sizes if you like, just adjust the cooking time accordingly.

Lightly oil a baking tray and sprinkle over the semolina. Put the shaped bread sticks on the tray and flavour with your chosen toppings. Bake in the oven for 15–20 minutes, or until golden and crispy. Transfer to a cooling rack and leave to cool. These can be stored in an airtight container for up to 1 month.

I'm always amazed at how good frozen broad beans are for this recipe, so don't worry if you can't get hold of fresh ones – at least it means you can make it year-round! Spend the time double shelling the beans once they are cooked – this gives a smooth, vibrant green spread.

Broad Bean and Roasted Garlic Spread

250 g/9 oz frozen or fresh broad beans

2 roasted garlic cloves (see page 134), roughly chopped

a small handful of fresh flat-leafed parsley

juice of ½ lemon

60 ml/2 fl oz extra virgin olive oil

salt and freshly ground black pepper

To serve

toasted sourdough bread, or Crostini (see page 23)

Manchego cheese

freshly ground black pepper

Makes about 250 g/9 oz

Bring a saucepan of water to the boil. Add the broad beans and bring back to the boil, then reduce the heat and simmer for 2–3 minutes, or until tender. Drain the broad beans and rinse them under running cold water until cool enough to handle. Remove the outer shell from the broad beans and put the vibrant green centres into the bowl of a food processor (this is a labour of love).

Add the garlic, parsley and lemon juice and whiz to combine. With the motor running, add the olive oil through the feed tube and continue blitzing to a smooth paste. Taste to season, then transfer to a bowl and refrigerate until ready to serve.

Serve on toasted sourdough or crostini with a few shavings of Manchego cheese on top and a good grind of black pepper. Keeps for 5–7 days.

Alioli is the Spanish version of aïoli, the rich, creamy, Italian garlic mayonnaise. Traditionally, in Catalonia it would include only garlic, oil and salt. For a slightly more subtle and smoky flavour, try using a bulb of Roasted Garlic (see page 134) instead of six garlic cloves.

Alioli

6 garlic cloves, peeled and finely chopped

½ teaspoon fine salt

2 large egg yolks

60 ml/2 fl oz light extra virgin olive oil

100–125 ml/3½– 4 fl oz vegetable oil, such as sunflower or canola oil

Makes about 300 ml/½ pint

Put the garlic and salt in a mortar and, using the pestle, grind to a paste. (Alternatively, use a large, heavy knife to mash and chop the garlic to a paste.) Put the garlic in a small food processor or blender, add the egg yolks and mix well. With the machine running, slowly add the combined oils, small quantities at a time, until the mixture is very thick.

Use immediately, or transfer to an airtight container or jar and refrigerate for up to 2 days.

These cold cocktail stick snacks are served in bars throughout Spain. Be inventive and try spearing your own combinations on to cocktail sticks. This is just one idea to get you started but Ham, Melon and Fig (see page 48) and Caramelised Onions Wrapped in Anchovies (see page 80) work on the same principle and are equally delicious. There's no end to the options!

Banderillas

12 cocktail sticks

12 whole small gherkins, or
3 large dill gherkins, each cut into 4

12 pearl (silverskin) onions, or baby pickled onions

12 pitted green olives

2 red pimiento peppers, cut into 12 squares

6 guindilla peppers, halved

Makes 12

Skewer one of each pickle with the pepper pieces, onions and olives on a cocktail stick in any order. Try varying the order for maximum aesthetic appeal.

The anchovy topping is quite salty so make sure you spread the paste thinly on the bread. The parsley and oil help break through the saltiness – and so does a glass of sherry.

Anchovy Toasts

30 g/1 oz finely grated Parmesan or Manchego cheese

1 garlic clove, peeled and crushed

a small handful of fresh flat-leafed parsley, finely chopped

30 g/1 oz tinned anchovy fillets in oil, drained and finely chopped

1–2 tablespoons extra virgin olive oil

freshly ground black pepper

1 loaf sourdough bread (or other bread)

Serves 4–6 as part of a selection of tapas

Combine all the ingredients, except the bread, in a small bowl and, using a fork, mash together to form a rough paste. Add a little extra olive oil if the mixture feels too dry to spread.

Preheat the grill to hot. Cut the bread into thin slices, about 5 mm/ ¼ inch thick. Using a knife, spread the paste over the bread slices in a thin layer until all the paste is used up or the desired number of toasts are made. (Any remaining mixture can be refrigerated for up to 3 days.)

Toast the bread under the grill for 3–4 minutes, or until the topping is bubbling and lightly golden. Serve warm, sliced into triangles or into long strips.

Crostini are the basis of many tapas in Spain. They are usually kept simple with a slice of ham or a wedge of cheese, and you are often handed them when you order a drink at the bar. These can be made in advance and stored in an airtight container for emergency situations.

Crostini

1 large baguette, or thinly sliced sourdough bread

4 tablespoons extra virgin olive oil

Makes 24–30

Preheat the oven to 180°C/350°F/mark 4. Using a bread knife, cut the baguette into 24–30 diagonal slices, about 1 cm/½ inch thick. Brush both sides of the bread with olive oil and place in a single layer on 1 or 2 baking trays.

Bake in the oven for 10–12 minutes, turning once, or until golden and crisp. Remove from the oven and cool completely.

Serve topped with your topping of choice. These can be stored in an airtight container for up to 1 month.

These can be filled with anything you like. Try adding rocket and roasted vegetables or, for a non-vegetarian version, Serrano ham. Impressive, but simple to make, this is a great storecupboard recipe and a great party stand-by. Manchego is a Spanish sheep's cheese.

Quesadillas

4 small tortilla breads

2 tablespoons extra virgin olive oil

150 g/5 oz Manchego cheese, thinly sliced

2–3 roasted red peppers (see page 134), peeled and cut into strips

salt and freshly ground black pepper

Makes 12–16

Using a pastry brush, brush one side of each tortilla with olive oil. Place 2 tortillas, unoiled-side up, on a large chopping board or work surface. Place half the cheese and pepper strips in an even layer on each tortilla, then season generously with salt and black pepper. Place the remaining tortillas on top with the oiled side up.

Preheat a large, non-stick frying pan until moderately hot. Cook the quesadillas one at a time. Carefully place the first one in the pan and cook for 2–3 minutes, or until the underside is golden and the cheese is starting to melt. Using a large palette knife or fish slice, carefully flip the quesadilla over and cook for a further 2–3 minutes. Remove from the pan and cook the second quesadilla in the same way.

Cut each quesadilla into 6–8 wedges and serve warm.

This is great served as part of a platter with some thinly sliced toasted breads, pickled gherkins, Banderillas (see page 20), Caramelised Fennel and Onion Relish (see page 14) and a few crisp chicory leaves. Make sure you buy fresh, plump and shiny-looking livers.

Chicken Liver Pâté

250 g/9 oz butter, plus extra to seal

1 small onion, peeled and chopped

300 g/11 oz chicken livers, trimmed

3 bacon rashers, chopped

1 sprig fresh thyme, leaves removed

100 ml/3½ fl oz fino (dry) sherry

salt and freshly ground black pepper

Serves 4–6 as part of a selection of tapas

Melt the butter in a large, non-stick frying pan and sauté the onion for 2–3 minutes, or until cooked and translucent but not browned. Add the chicken livers, bacon and thyme and sauté until the chicken livers are cooked but still slightly pink in the centre and the bacon is browned – 2–3 minutes.

Increase the heat and add the sherry so that it sizzles and the alcohol burns off. Remove from the heat and season generously.

Transfer the mixture to a food processor and whiz to a smooth paste. Pack the mixture into small ramekins or dishes and smooth off the surface, then place a thyme sprig and some coarsely ground black pepper in the centre of each. Melt a little extra butter in a small saucepan and pour a thin layer evenly over the pâté. Allow to cool, then refrigerate until the butter has set. Use within 5 days.

The simplicity of this dish means that it must be made with only the best-quality tomatoes and extra virgin olive oil. Anything sub-standard will simply disappoint. In Andalusia, in the south of Spain, they make a version where the tomatoes are blanched, peeled and blended to a smooth, frothy and spoonable consistency that can be spread on to toasted bread as well.

Catalan Tomato Bread

1 small loaf crusty, country-style white bread (not ciabatta)

2 garlic cloves, peeled

about 4 very ripe vine-ripened tomatoes

extra virgin olive oil

sea salt

Makes 8 slices

Preheat the grill. Slice the bread into 8 slices about 1.5 cm/¾ inch thick and lightly toast both sides. Rub the garlic over one side of each slice, then generously rub a tomato half over each slice so that lots of juice and seeds remain.

Transfer to a plate, drizzle with the olive oil, sprinkle with sea salt and serve.

An alternative to humous that in my mind is even more delicious. When served with poached fish or fried sausages, it doubles up as an alternative to mash.

White Bean and Lemon Spread

400 g/14 oz cooked butter beans, rinsed and well drained

2 garlic cloves, peeled and crushed

zest and juice of 1 large lemon

1 teaspoon fine salt

50–75 ml/2–3 fl oz extra virgin olive oil

1 small bunch of fresh flat-leafed parsley, chopped (optional)

freshly ground black pepper

To serve

Crostini (see page 23)

Roasted Cherry Tomatoes (see page 135)

Makes about 500 g/1 lb 2 oz

Put the butter beans, garlic, lemon zest and juice, salt and black pepper in a food processor and whiz for about 30 seconds. With the machine running, pour in the olive oil through the feed tube until it forms a smooth paste. Stir in the parsley, if using.

Serve spread on crostini and topped with a roasted cherry tomato.

This sweet and smoky salsa is delicious served with meat, particularly as a dipping salsa for pork or beef skewers. For a more simple alternative, serve with Crostini (see page 23) or crusty bread.

Sweet Chilli and Red Pepper Salsa

2 roasted red peppers (see page 134), peeled and deseeded

1 red onion, peeled and very finely diced

2–3 sweet red chillies, deseeded and finely chopped

1 garlic clove, peeled and crushed

½ teaspoon Spanish sweet smoked paprika

100 ml/3½ fl oz extra virgin olive oil

juice of ½ lemon

a small handful of fresh flat-leafed parsley, roughly chopped

salt and freshly ground black pepper

Makes about 250 g/9 oz

Chop the roasted peppers into fine dice and put into a bowl. Add all the remaining ingredients and mix well to combine. Taste and season accordingly. Use within 5–7 days.

Why buy it when you can make your own? Okay, I know it's not always the right season, but when it is you can just make double and stock up for the year – it's much more satisfying and cost effective than shop-bought.

Quince Paste (Membrillo)

2 kg/4¼ lb quinces, washed, cored and quartered

500 ml/17 fl oz water

juice of 1 lemon

caster sugar

1 cinnamon stick

Makes 1.25 kg/2½ lb

Put the quinces in a saucepan with the water and lemon juice. Bring to the boil, then reduce the heat and simmer for 45–60 minutes, until they are soft.

Purée the fruit in a food processor, or push through a sieve. Weigh the puréed fruit and transfer the purée with an equal weight of sugar and the cinnamon stick to a clean, heavy-based saucepan.

Cook the paste over a low heat, stirring, until the mixture thickens and you can hardly move the spoon through it – this will take about 1 hour. Keep stirring particularly when the mixture thickens so that it doesn't burn. The mixture will take on a pink colour as it cooks. Be careful of it spitting.

Line a slice tin or shallow baking tray with greaseproof paper and spread the mixture over it. Turn the oven to its lowest possible temperature and leave the mixture in there for 12 hours, or overnight. Alternatively, store in another warm place for 12 hours. The paste should be stored in an airtight container and will last for up to 12 months.

This light, buttery pastry is a great way to impress your guests.
However, if time is limited, a great substitute is ready-made puff
pastry from your local supermarket.

Empanada Pastry

500 g/1 lb 2 oz plain flour, plus extra for dusting

½ teaspoon fine salt

approximately 250 ml/8 fl oz water

250 g/9 oz butter, at room temperature

Makes 750 g/1½ lb

Mix the flour with the salt in a large bowl and make a well in the centre.
Gradually mix in enough water to make a smooth, workable dough.
Knead the dough for 8–10 minutes, then cover and chill for at least
30 minutes.

Roll the dough out on a large, lightly floured, flat surface, or floured
board, into a rectangle about 45 x 30 cm/17½ x 12 inches and
5 mm/¼ inch thick. Spread the butter evenly over the dough and
fold each short edge into the centre, then the whole thing in half
again, so that it is four layers thick. Cover and refrigerate for a further
30 minutes.

After 30 minutes, roll the dough out again to 45 x 30 cm/17½ x
12 inches and again fold into four, then return it to the fridge for a
final 30 minutes. The dough is then ready to use.

Roll the dough out so that it is about 2.5 mm/⅛ inch thick and cut it
into about 10 cm/4 inch circles for individual empanadas, or 2 large
rounds for Galician-style empanadas. Return them to the fridge and
work with only a few at a time. Fill and cook as directed in the recipe.

Meat & Chicken

These bite-sized, fried meatballs are found throughout Spain served with a variety of different sauces. These are albondigas caseras – meatballs served with a tomato, onion and pepper sauce.

Spanish Meatballs (Albondigas)

250 g/9 oz (about 4) good-quality pork sausages

400 g/14 oz lean beef mince

¼–½ teaspoon dried chilli flakes

1 garlic clove, peeled and crushed

1 small bunch fresh flat-leafed parsley, finely chopped, plus extra to serve

1 medium onion, peeled and very finely chopped

1–2 tablespoons plain flour

2 tablespoons extra virgin olive oil

1 small red pepper, deseeded and finely diced

½ teaspoon Spanish sweet smoked paprika

700 g/1½ lb jar of passata (tomato pulp)

salt and freshly ground black pepper

Serves 4–6 as part of a selection of tapas

Squeeze the sausage meat from its casings into a large mixing bowl. Add the beef mince, chilli flakes, garlic, parsley and half the chopped onion and mix thoroughly (it is easiest using your hands, but you can use a fork if you prefer). Season the mixture generously with salt and black pepper.

Sprinkle the flour over a chopping board and lightly flour your hands. Take heaped teaspoons of the mixture and shape into walnut-sized balls until all the mixture has been used.

Preheat the oven to 190°C/375°F/mark 5. Heat 1 tablespoon of the olive oil in a large, non-stick frying pan and fry the meatballs until brown all over. As they brown, transfer them to a large ovenproof dish that can hold them in a single layer.

Heat the remaining tablespoon of oil in the same frying pan. Add the remaining onion, the diced pepper and paprika and sauté for about 2–3 minutes. Stir in the passata, bring to the boil and cook for a further 3 minutes. Season to taste.

Pour the sauce over the meatballs and cook, uncovered, in the oven for 30–35 minutes, or until lightly browned, turning once during cooking.

Serve the meatballs warm with cocktail sticks.

Thighs are the moist, dark meat of the chicken. It is sometimes a good idea to trim back the skin because it can be quite fatty. Thighs are also easily de-boned and can be stuffed and then secured with a couple of cocktail sticks before being cooked in the same way as below. If stuffed, they will need a little longer cooking – do the skewer test to ensure they're cooked through.

Crispy Garlic Chicken Pieces

1 tablespoon extra virgin olive oil

1 kg/2¼ lb small chicken thighs, skin on

1 teaspoon Spanish hot smoked paprika

2 teaspoons dried oregano or thyme, or a mixture

3 large garlic cloves, peeled and crushed

Serves 6 as part of a selection of tapas

Preheat the oven to 200°C/400°F/mark 6. Heat the olive oil in a large, non-stick frying pan until hot. Add all the chicken pieces and the paprika and sauté for 4–5 minutes, or until starting to colour.

Add the dried herbs and garlic and continue frying for a further 5–7 minutes, stirring regularly, or until the chicken is starting to turn crispy and is golden brown all over.

Transfer to a baking dish and cook in the oven for 15–20 minutes, or until the chicken is cooked and no pink juices run when a skewer is inserted into the thickest part of the flesh. Serve hot, warm, or cold.

These little bread towers are just one of the many combinations that can be secured together with a cocktail stick and served as a tapa. In Granada I was once served a piece of very thinly sliced roast pork on fresh white baguette – simple as that and absolutely delicious!

Marinated Pork and Membrillo Tapas

300–350 g/11–12 oz pork fillet, sliced into approximately 20 x 1 cm/½ inch thick rounds

1 small loaf sourdough or rye bread

150 g/5 oz Quince Paste (Membrillo, see page 30)

about 20 green olives stuffed with pimiento

For the marinade

2 tablespoons extra virgin olive oil

2 tablespoons fino (dry) sherry

1 teaspoon Spanish sweet smoked paprika

1 tablespoon fresh thyme leaves

1 garlic clove, peeled and crushed

juice of 1 small orange

Makes about 20

Combine all the marinade ingredients in a medium-sized bowl. Add the sliced pork and leave to marinate for at least 2 hours, or up to 24 hours.

While the pork is marinating, prepare the bread. Preheat the grill. Slice the loaf into approximately 20 x 1 cm/½ inch thick slices and toast under the grill on both sides until just golden. Cool, cut into finger food-sized pieces and set aside in an airtight container or bag until ready to serve.

Just before serving, heat a large, non-stick frying pan to medium heat. Cook the pork slices for 1–2 minutes on each side, or until golden and cooked through.

Place one pork slice on each piece of bread, top with a cube of membrillo and an olive and secure with a cocktail stick. Serve within the hour if possible.

This is one of life's little indulgences. Juicy and succulent pork belly is not a tapa to eat every night if you're concerned about your heart. Pork belly has an equal proportion of fat and meat and this recipe is equally good cooked on the barbecue as it is in the oven.

Fennel and Rosemary Roasted Pork Belly

500 g/1 lb 2 oz streaky pork slices, or pork belly (without rind), cut into 6–8 strips

2 sprigs fresh rosemary, finely chopped

2 garlic cloves, peeled and crushed

1 tablespoon fennel seeds

1 tablespoon extra virgin olive oil

2 teaspoons sea salt

Makes 12–24

Preheat the oven to 200°C/400°F/mark 6. Place the pork in a single layer in a large roasting dish and set aside while you prepare the coating.

Combine the rosemary, garlic, fennel seeds and olive oil in a small bowl. Using your hands, rub the mixture over the pork slices, then sprinkle generously with the salt.

Cook in the oven for about 30 minutes, turning once, until golden and crispy and the pork is cooked through.

Remove from the oven and cut each strip into 2–3 pieces. Serve warm with cocktail sticks.

This is one of those tapas that comes into the category of a main meal downsized!

40 Mini Chorizo Sausages with White Bean Mash

200 g/7 oz cooked and drained white beans, such as butter or cannellini

1 garlic clove, peeled and crushed

50 ml/2 fl oz extra virgin olive oil

12 (about 225 g/8 oz) mini cooking chorizo sausages

1 onion, peeled and very finely sliced

1 teaspoon caster sugar

50 ml/2 fl oz Rioja, or other red wine

salt and freshly ground black pepper

Serves 4–6 as part of a selection of tapas

Prepare the white bean mash first. Put the cooked beans in a food processor with the garlic and whiz several times. With the motor still running, pour the oil through the feed tube to form a slightly smooth mash. Taste and season accordingly, then put to one side.

Heat a large, non-stick frying pan and cook the chorizo, turning frequently, over a medium-hot heat until the oils are released – about 4–5 minutes. Add the onion and sugar and sauté in the oil until the onion is soft and starting to caramelise. With the heat hot, add the wine so that it sizzles and allows the alcohol to burn off. Stir for a further couple of minutes until it thickens, then remove from the heat.

When ready to serve, transfer the white bean mash to a heatproof bowl and microwave on High for 3 minutes, stirring once. Alternatively, heat 1 tablespoon of oil in a pan and sauté the mash until warmed through.

Place a small pile of white bean mash on each plate, top with two or three sausages and serve warm.

These little morsels are quite addictive, so be careful not to eat too many or you won't fit in any other tapas.

Chicken and Blue Cheese Croquettes

50 g/2 oz butter

75 g/3 oz plain flour

400 ml/14 fl oz milk

50 g/2 oz blue cheese, crumbled

1 tablespoon extra virgin olive oil

1 small onion, peeled and finely chopped

200 g/7 oz finely chopped chicken breast

1 tablespoon finely chopped fresh chives

1 egg, beaten

75 g/3 oz dried breadcrumbs

vegetable or sunflower oil, for deep-frying

freshly ground black pepper

Makes 20

Melt the butter in a heavy-based saucepan. Stir in the flour and cook, stirring, until it changes colour slightly. Remove from the heat, add a little of the milk and, using a whisk, stir to combine. Slowly stir in the remaining milk until smooth, then return to the heat and continue stirring until the mixture becomes very thick. Stir in the cheese and set aside.

Heat the olive oil in a small, non-stick frying pan and sauté the onion until cooked and translucent but not browned. Add the chicken and continue cooking for a further 5–7 minutes, or until the chicken is thoroughly cooked. Stir the chicken mixture into the cheese sauce along with the chives. Taste and season accordingly. Pour into a deep-sided baking dish or tray and refrigerate for at least 2 hours.

Cut the mixture into 20 and shape into croquettes. Dip them, one at a time, in the beaten egg, then roll them in the breadcrumbs. They can be refrigerated at this stage until you are ready to cook them.

Heat the vegetable or sunflower oil in a heavy-based saucepan to 190°C/375°F, or until a small cube of bread turns golden in about 30 seconds. Deep-fry the croquettes for 3–4 minutes, or until golden brown and hot through. Remove with a slotted spoon and drain on kitchen paper. Serve hot.

Croquettes require a very thick béchamel sauce, which is mixed with very finely chopped meat and left to chill. The mixture then becomes firm enough to shape into small sausage shapes or balls before being deep-fried and served hot.

Ham Croquettes

50 g/2 oz butter

75 g/3 oz plain flour

400 ml/14 fl oz milk

50 g/2 oz Cheddar or Manchego cheese, cut into small cubes

1 tablespoon extra virgin olive oil

1 small onion, peeled and finely chopped

100 g/3½ oz Serrano ham, finely chopped

1 egg, beaten

75 g/3 oz dried breadcrumbs

vegetable or sunflower oil, for deep-frying

freshly ground black pepper

Makes 20

Melt the butter in a heavy-based saucepan. Stir in the flour and cook, stirring, until it changes colour slightly – this means the roux is cooked. Remove from the heat, add a little of the milk and, using a whisk, stir to combine. Slowly stir in the remaining milk until smooth, then return the pan to the heat and continue stirring until the mixture becomes very thick. Stir in the cheese and set aside.

Heat the olive oil in a small, non-stick frying pan and sauté the onion for 2–3 minutes, or until cooked and translucent but not browned. Stir in the ham and remove from the heat. Stir the ham mixture into the white sauce, season with black pepper, then pour into a deep-sided baking dish or tray and refrigerate for at least 2 hours.

Cut the mixture into 20 and shape into croquettes. Dip them, one at a time, in the beaten egg, then roll them in the breadcrumbs. They can be refrigerated at this stage until you are ready to cook them.

Heat the vegetable or sunflower oil in a heavy-based saucepan to 190°C/375°F, or until a small cube of bread turns golden in about 30 seconds. Deep-fry the croquettes in batches for 3–4 minutes each batch, or until golden brown and hot through. Remove with a slotted spoon and drain on kitchen paper. Serve hot.

These have become a very popular party snack and work well as part of a selection of tapas. I like them with something fresh and crisp such as my Valencia Orange, Fennel and Black Olive Salad (see page 124), but most of my friends seem to like them just the way they are.

Paprika-Glazed Pork Sausages

2 tablespoons extra virgin olive oil

2 tablespoons runny honey

1 tablespoon tomato paste

2 tablespoons soy sauce

1–2 teaspoons Spanish hot smoked paprika, to taste

500 g/1 lb 2 oz (24–30) cocktail pork sausages

2 teaspoons sesame seeds

Serves 4–6 as part of a selection of tapas

Preheat the oven to 180°C/350°F/mark 4. Combine the olive oil, honey, tomato paste, soy sauce and paprika in a large bowl. Add the sausages and mix to coat.

Put the sausages and most of the glaze on to a baking tray or ovenproof dish and cook in the oven for 12–15 minutes, basting and turning once or twice during cooking. Stir the sesame seeds in after about 10 minutes. The sausages should be golden, sticky and slightly caramelised.

Serve warm with cocktail sticks.

The use of intensely flavoured and sticky pomegranate molasses adds a unique flavour to this dish and tenderises the meat, giving a Moorish result.

Pomegranate and Yoghurt-Marinated Lamb Skewers

4 tablespoons plain
unsweetened yoghurt

1 tablespoon
pomegranate molasses

1 teaspoon
ground cumin

500 g/1 lb 2 oz lamb
leg steaks, cut into
2.5–3 cm/1–1¼
inch cubes

1 pomegranate

a small handful of
fresh flat-leafed
parsley, chopped

freshly ground
black pepper

12 small skewers
(if wooden, soaked in
water for 2–24 hours)

Makes 12

Combine the yoghurt, molasses and cumin in a bowl and season generously with black pepper. Pour the marinade over the lamb and stir until evenly and well coated. Cover and refrigerate for at least 1 hour, or up to 24 hours.

Just before you are ready to cook the skewers, preheat the oven to 200°C/400°F/mark 6. Thread 3–4 lamb pieces on to each skewer and place on a large, foil-lined baking tray.

Cook the skewers in the oven for 8–12 minutes, turning once or twice, or until golden and the lamb is cooked to your desired doneness.

Meanwhile, remove the seeds from the pomegranate and take off any white pith.

Serve the lamb warm sprinkled with pomegranate seeds and the chopped parsley.

These make a nice change from the usual asparagus wrapped in jamon or prosciutto. I love the way the leeks retain a little bit of crunch when you bite into them.

This is a selection of dried and cured meats. Choose amounts depending on how many people you are feeding. The following is a guide for 6–8 people.

Baby Leeks Wrapped in Jamon

12 baby leeks

6 slices (about 75 g/ 3 oz) of jamon or prosciutto

1 tablespoon extra virgin olive oil

sea salt and freshly ground black pepper

Makes 12

Preheat the oven to 180°C/350°F/gas mark 4. Using a small knife, make a slit down the side of each leek just deep enough to remove the outer leaf. Trim both ends on an angle and wash the leek well to remove any dirt.

Wrap the central part of each leek in half a slice of jamon or prosciutto and place on a baking tray. Drizzle over the olive oil and season generously with salt and black pepper.

Cook in the oven for 10–12 minutes, or until the leeks are soft and lightly browned. Serve warm.

Spanish Charcuterie Platter

75–100 g/3–3½ oz thinly sliced Serrano ham

75–100 g/3–3½ oz thinly sliced cooked chorizo sausage

75–100 g/3–3½ oz thinly sliced lomo (pork loin)

caperberries

crusty bread or Crostini (see page 23)

extra virgin olive oil

Serves 6–8

Arrange the thinly sliced meats on a large platter and garnish with a few caperberries. Serve a plate of crusty or toasted breads on the side with some extra virgin olive oil for drizzling.

I remember sitting up at a bar in Granada at the end of a very long night. My friend Ian had dragged us around all the oldest and best bars in town and somehow there was still room for this little treat – you'll see why!

Complete simplicity but absolutely delicious, the saltiness of the ham offsets the juiciness and sweetness of the melon and fig.

Peas and Broad Beans with Pancetta

150 g/5 oz freshly shelled peas

150 g/5 oz freshly shelled broad beans

2 tablespoons extra virgin olive oil

3 shallots, peeled and finely chopped

150 g/5 oz pancetta cubes

1 large sprig fresh rosemary, finely chopped

salt and freshly ground black pepper

Serves 4–6 as part of a selection of tapas

Bring a large saucepan of water to the boil and cook the peas and broad beans for 3–4 minutes, or until just cooked. Drain then set aside.

Heat the olive oil in a large, non-stick frying pan and sauté the shallots and pancetta until golden brown. Stir in the rosemary and sauté for a further minute.

Remove from the heat, stir in the peas and broad beans and season to taste with salt and black pepper. Serve warm.

Ham, Melon and Fig

12 cocktail sticks

2 slices of Serrano ham, cut into 5 cm/ 2 inch slices

12 small cubes (about 100 g/3½ oz) honeydew melon

3 figs, each cut into quarters

Makes 12

Wrap one slice of ham around each cube of melon and skewer on to a cocktail stick. Skewer a piece of fig on each and serve.

Red peppers are generally juicier and sweeter that green peppers
and so are often the preferred choice for roasting. Ramiro peppers
are the long ones, sometimes called Hungarian peppers; however,
regular sweet peppers can also be used in this recipe.

Ramiro Peppers Stuffed with Pork and Rosemary

3 large, red Ramiro peppers, 250–300 g/ 9–11 oz total weight

1 tablespoon extra virgin olive oil

1 medium onion, peeled and finely diced

1 garlic clove, peeled and crushed

2 sprigs fresh rosemary, finely chopped (about 1 tablespoon chopped)

¼ teaspoon dried chilli flakes

450 g/1 lb pork mince

1 tablespoon tomato paste

75 ml/3 fl oz sweet Madeira

400 g/14 oz tin chopped tomatoes

salt and freshly ground black pepper

Makes 6 tapas-sized portions

Cut the peppers in half lengthways and place, cut-side up, on a baking tray, then set aside.

Heat the olive oil in a large, non-stick frying pan and sauté the onion for 2–3 minutes, or until translucent but not browned. Add the garlic, rosemary and chilli flakes and sauté for a further minute. Add the pork mince, increase the heat and cook until the mince is browned and cooked, breaking it up with a wooden fork or spoon as you go. When the meat has browned, lower the heat and stir in the tomato paste and then the Madeira. Cook until all the liquid has evaporated, then add the tomatoes and cook for a further 10 minutes. Season and set aside to cool slightly.

Preheat the oven to 190°C/375°F/mark 5. Spoon the mixture into the pepper halves and bake in the oven for about 15 minutes, or until the peppers are cooked and the filling lightly golden on top. Serve warm or cool.

This is a chunky and hearty salad that can be served warm or cold. The juices from the sausages give the dish a golden glow and spicy note. Make sure you get the potatoes and chorizo golden and crispy and then the dish is easily eaten with cocktail sticks instead of a fork.

Crispy Chorizo and New Potatoes

500 g /1 lb 2 oz new potatoes, scrubbed

3 (about 300 g/11 oz) cooking chorizo sausages chopped into 1 cm/½ inch slices

2 sprigs fresh rosemary, leaves chopped finely

2 tablespoons dry Madeira

Serves 4–6 as part of a selection of tapas

Boil the potatoes for 8–10 minutes, or until cooked but still firm. Remove from the heat and cool them under running cold water, then cut them in half lengthways on the diagonal and set aside.

Heat a large, non-stick frying pan to hot and cook the chorizo for 2–3 minutes, or until the oils are released. Add the potatoes and rosemary and cook, stirring frequently, over a high heat for a further 2–3 minutes, or until golden and crispy.

Reduce the heat and add the Madeira. Stir and leave to caramelise and brown for a further 2–3 minutes, stirring occasionally.

Serve warm with cocktail sticks, or as a salad.

Chillies play an important role in Spanish cooking, adding to dishes not only heat but also distinct flavours. This tapa uses the chillies and seeds for heat and the paprika, a chilli derivative, for flavour.

Peri Peri Chicken Nibbles

24 chicken wings

2–3 red chillies, stems removed, deseeded and roughly chopped

4 tablespoons cider vinegar

4 tablespoons extra virgin olive oil

1 tablespoon cayenne pepper

2 garlic cloves, peeled and crushed

1 tablespoon Spanish hot smoked paprika

1 teaspoon fine salt

Makes 24 nibbles

Using poultry shears or sharp kitchen scissors, cut the tips from the chicken wings, through the joint. Put all the wings in a large plastic bag or non-metallic bowl and set aside.

To prepare the marinade, put all the remaining ingredients in a food processor or blender and whiz to a smooth paste. Place the marinade over the chicken and mix well until the chicken is evenly coated. Cover and refrigerate for at least 30 minutes, or up to 24 hours.

When you are ready to cook the chicken, preheat the oven to 220°C/425°F/mark 7. Place the chicken on a baking tray and cook in the oven for 15–20 minutes, or until cooked through and no pink juices are released when a skewer is inserted into the thickest part of the flesh.

Serve warm or cold with plenty of paper napkins.

In literal terms, empanadas are actually large pies and empanadillas are smaller pies. They can come with a range of fillings from pork to seafood and egg to vegetable. Spicy chicken is always a party pleaser!

Spicy Chicken Empanadas

1 quantity Empanada Pastry (see page 31), or 500 g/1 lb 2 oz bought puff pastry

1 tablespoon extra virgin olive oil

1 small onion, peeled and very finely chopped

1 garlic clove, peeled and crushed

1 teaspoon dried chilli flakes

1 teaspoon ground cumin

½ teaspoon ground coriander

½ teaspoon ground cinnamon

300 g/11 oz (about 2 breasts) chicken breast meat, finely chopped

125 ml/4 fl oz passata (tomato pulp)

plain flour, for dusting

30 g/1 oz butter, melted

salt and freshly ground black pepper

Makes 24–30

Prepare the pastry and refrigerate until ready to assemble.

Heat the olive oil in a non-stick frying pan and sauté the onion for about 2 minutes, or until translucent but not browned. Add the garlic, chilli flakes, ground cumin, coriander and cinnamon and sauté for a further minute. Add the chicken, increase the heat and cook until the meat is browned.

Lower the heat and stir in the passata, then cook for a further 3–4 minutes, or until the chicken is cooked and the mixture not too wet. Season to taste.

When you are ready to cook the empanadas, preheat the oven to 200°C/400°F/mark 6. Roll the pastry out on a lightly floured surface to 3–4 mm/¼ inch thick and, using a 9–10 cm/3¾–4 inch round cutter, cut out circles. Place a heaped teaspoon of the filling on one half of each round of pastry. Dip your finger in water and slightly dampen the pastry edges (to help them stick), then fold the pastry over the filling to make a half-moon shape. To seal the empanadas, pinch the edges of the pastry firmly together, then press down on the edges with the prongs of a fork to finish.

Brush the empanadas with melted butter and bake in the oven for 15–18 minutes, or until golden and puffed. Serve hot or warm.

Empanadas are traditionally deep-fried, but I prefer the slightly
healthier option of baking the parcels instead.

Pork Empanadas

1 quantity Empanada
Pastry (see page 31),
or 500 g/1 lb 2 oz
bought puff pastry

1 tablespoon extra
virgin olive oil

1 small onion, peeled
and finely diced

1 garlic clove,
peeled and crushed

1 sprig fresh
rosemary, finely
chopped (about
½ tablespoon
chopped)

¼ teaspoon dried
chilli flakes

200 g/7 oz
pork mince

1 tablespoon
tomato paste

2 tablespoons
dry Madeira

plain flour, for dusting

30 g/1 oz
butter, melted

salt and freshly
ground black pepper

Makes 30–36

Prepare the pastry and refrigerate until ready to assemble.

Heat the olive oil in a non-stick frying pan and sauté the onion for
about 2 minutes, or until translucent but not browned. Add the garlic,
rosemary and chilli flakes and sauté for a further minute. Add the pork
mince, increase the heat and cook until the mince is browned and
cooked, breaking it up with a wooden fork or spoon as you go. When
the meat has browned, lower the heat and stir in the tomato paste,
then add the Madeira and season to taste. Cook until all the liquid has
evaporated, then take off the heat and leave to cool.

When you are ready to cook the empanadas, preheat the oven to
200°C/400°F/mark 6. Roll the pastry out on a lightly floured surface to
3–4 mm/¼ inch thick and, using a 9–10 cm/3¾–4 inch round cutter,
cut out circles.

Place a heaped teaspoon of the filling on one half of each round of
pastry. Dip your finger in water and slightly dampen the pastry edges
(to help them stick), then fold the pastry over the filling to make a half-
moon shape. To seal the empanadas, pinch the edges of the pastry
firmly together, then press down on the edges with the prongs of a fork
to finish.

Brush the empanadas with melted butter and bake in the oven for
15–18 minutes, or until golden and puffed. Serve hot or warm.

These are like devils-on-horseback, except I use a date instead of a prune. You must eat these while they are still warm and the dates are soft and moist from the still-hot bacon juices. As an alternative, try stuffing the dates with a small cube of blue cheese or mozzarella.

Dates Wrapped in Bacon

12 large (about 200 g/7 oz) dates (I use Medjool)

12 blanched almonds

6 (about 125 g/4 oz) streaky bacon rashers

Makes 12

Preheat the oven to 200°C/400°F/mark 6. Line a baking tray with foil.

Using a small knife, make a slit down one side of each date and remove the stone. Place one almond inside each date and push to close. Cut each slice of bacon in half through the middle and wrap one piece of bacon around each date. Use a cocktail stick to secure the bacon in place.

Put the wrapped dates on the baking tray and cook for 12–15 minutes, turning once, until the bacon is golden brown and crispy. Serve warm.

This recipe has Moorish influences coming through, with saffron and cinnamon being important flavours in the dish. If you like, you can use baby aubergines – this just becomes a little more fiddly when scooping out the aubergine flesh. Likewise, this filling can be used to stuff peppers, hollowed-out courgette halves, or tomatoes – just adjust the cooking time depending on the vegetable you choose.

Aubergines Stuffed with Saffron Minced Lamb

1 tablespoon extra virgin olive oil

1 medium onion, peeled and finely chopped

400 g/14 oz lamb mince

200 ml/7 fl oz passata (tomato pulp), or ½ x 400 g/14 oz tin chopped tomatoes

½–1 teaspoon ground cinnamon

2 pinches of saffron threads

100 g/3½ oz stuffed green olives, of your choice, roughly chopped

4 small aubergines, 125–150 g/4–5 oz each

Makes 8 tapas-sized portions

Heat the olive oil in a large, non-stick frying pan and sauté the onion for 2–3 minutes, or until soft and translucent but not browned. Add the lamb mince and cook, breaking it up, for 7–10 minutes, or until browned and the juices have evaporated.

Stir in the passata or tomatoes, the cinnamon, saffron and olives and continue to simmer for a further 10–12 minutes.

While the mince mixture is cooking, preheat the oven to 200°C/400°F/mark 6 and prepare the aubergines. Cut each in half lengthways and scoop out the flesh. Finely chop the flesh and add to the mince mixture for at least the last 5 minutes of cooking. Place the aubergine shells, cut-side up, on a baking tray.

When the mince is cooked, fill the aubergine shells with the mince mixture and bake for 12–15 minutes, or until browned and the aubergine is soft. Serve hot, warm or cold.

The best chorizo contains as much as 95 per cent pork along with salt, garlic and paprika to give it its pronounced red colour. It is cured either to a hard sausage consistency, to be sliced and eaten as it is, or to a softer consistency to use in cooking. The variety to choose for this tapa is the one that has not been completely cured and still requires cooking before eating. Depending on your preference, you can choose from mild, sweet, or spicy varieties.

Chorizo in Red Wine

3 (about 300 g/11 oz) cooking chorizo sausages, sliced into 2.5 cm/1 inch chunks

Heat a large, non-stick frying pan and add the chorizo. Sauté for 3–4 minutes, or until the juices start to release and the chorizo starts to brown.

50 ml/2 fl oz Rioja, or other red wine, or use sherry or Madeira

When the chorizo is crispy and golden, add the wine, increase the heat and sauté for a further couple of minutes until the juices start to caramelise and thicken.

Serves 4–6 as part of a selection of tapas

Serve immediately with cocktail sticks.

For a more succulent and tender result, buy mini-chicken
fillets rather than chopping chicken breasts into smaller pieces.
The aubergines add a subtle meaty-like texture to this dish.

Mini Mediterranean Chicken Fillets

1 large aubergine

1 tablespoon extra
virgin olive oil

400 g/14 oz (about 8)
mini chicken fillets, or
chicken breasts

1 teaspoon Spanish
hot smoked paprika

250 g/9 oz passata
(tomato pulp)

100 g/3½ oz
pimiento-stuffed
green olives

*Serves 4–6 as part of
a selection of tapas*

Preheat the oven to 200°C/400°F/mark 6. Rub the aubergine with about
1 teaspoon of the olive oil and bake in the oven for 25–30 minutes, or
until soft and cooked. Remove from the oven and set aside until cool
enough to handle, then peel the aubergine and chop into large chunks.
Reduce the oven temperature to 180°C/350°F/mark 4.

Meanwhile, if using chicken breasts, slice each one into 3–4 pieces.
Heat the remaining oil in a large, non-stick frying pan and cook the
chicken for 2–3 minutes until golden brown. Add the paprika and stir
to combine, then add the passata, aubergine and olives and cook for a
further 2–3 minutes.

Transfer to an ovenproof dish and cook in the oven for 15 minutes.
Serve hot or warm.

A Galician empanada is just one large pie cut into wedges, rather than individual crescents – somewhat like a calzone, except it's made using pastry. If you have the time, then make your own pastry – there's nothing more rewarding!

Galician-Style Chicken Empanada

1 quantity Empanada Pastry (see page 31), or 750 g/1 lb 10 oz bought puff pastry

2 tablespoons extra virgin olive oil

1 onion, peeled and finely chopped

1 red pepper, deseeded and finely diced

1 teaspoon cumin seeds

400 g/14 oz chicken breasts, roughly chopped into small pieces

1–2 teaspoons harissa (optional)

½–1 teaspoon fine salt

1 small bunch of fresh coriander, chopped

plain flour, for dusting

Makes 12 tapas-sized portions

Prepare the pastry as on page 31 and refrigerate until ready to assemble.

Heat the olive oil in a large, non-stick frying pan and sauté the onion for 3–4 minutes, or until translucent and soft. Add the diced pepper and cumin seeds and sauté for a further minute. Increase the heat, add the chicken and continue cooking, stirring frequently, until the chicken is cooked – this will take 5–7 minutes. Stir in the harissa paste and salt during the last few minutes of cooking. Stir in the coriander and set aside to cool completely.

When you are ready to assemble the empanada, preheat the oven to 220°C/425°F/mark 7. Roll the pastry out on a lightly floured surface to one large rectangle, about 3–4mm/¼ inch thick, and cut around a plate, about 30 cm/12 inches in diameter, to give you two equal-sized circles. Place one on a large, lightly floured baking tray. Spread the filling over evenly, then place the second circle on top. Using your fingers, crimp around the edges to seal.

Bake in the oven for 15–20 minutes, or until golden brown. Leave to cool slightly, then cut into wedges to serve. This can also be served cold.

Pork spare ribs are one of the least expensive cuts from the pig and make a great tapa that seems to appeal to young and old alike. Try cooking these on the barbecue for a slightly smoky and charred taste, but have lots of kitchen paper handy for all those sticky fingers!

To me, these pork skewers, with a splash of sherry and a dash of paprika, sum up the essence of Spanish tapas. Simple yet hearty, they are a party pleaser every time and are delicious served with a glass of chilled beer or fino sherry.

Sherry-Marinated Pork Ribs

500 g/1 lb 2 oz (12–15) mini pork ribs

For the marinade

2 tablespoons runny honey, plus extra to drizzle

1 tablespoon extra virgin olive oil

50 ml/2 fl oz dry sherry

1 teaspoon Spanish hot smoked paprika

2 tablespoons tomato paste

1 garlic clove, peeled and crushed

2 sprigs fresh thyme, leaves removed

Serves 4–6 as part of a selection of tapas

If the ribs are still in a rack, cut them into individual ribs, place in a large, non-metallic bowl and set aside.

Combine all the marinade ingredients in a bowl and pour over the ribs. Mix well to coat, then cover and refrigerate for 4–24 hours, turning occasionally.

When you are ready to cook, preheat the oven to 220°C/425°F/mark 7. Remove the ribs from the marinade and place in a single layer on a baking tray. Drizzle all over with a little extra honey. Cook in the oven for 18–20 minutes, turning and basting once or twice, until sticky and slightly charred. Serve immediately.

Marinated Pork Skewers (Pinchos Morunos)

600 g/1 lb 5½ oz pork fillet, cut into approximately 3 cm/1¼ inch cubes

12 short bamboo skewers, soaked in water for 2–24 hours

For the marinade

1 teaspoon cumin seeds

1 teaspoon fennel seeds

½ teaspoon Spanish hot smoked paprika

1 garlic clove, peeled and crushed

2 tablespoons extra virgin olive oil

1 tablespoon fino (dry) sherry

Serves 4–6 as part of a selection of tapas

Combine all the marinade ingredients in a large bowl. Add the pork and toss well to coat, then cover and leave to marinate for at least 1 hour, or up to 24 hours.

When ready to cook, preheat the grill to hot. Thread 3–4 cubes of pork on to each skewer and place on a foil-lined baking tray. Grill for 5 minutes on one side, then turn and grill for a further 3–4 minutes, or until golden, aromatic and the pork is cooked through.

Serve warm.

The word 'sherry' has become so generic over the decades that the distinctive characteristics of many noble styles such as fino, manzanilla, amontillado, oloroso and Pedro Ximenez have often been disregarded. It is important to familiarise yourself with the spectrum of flavours that each style contains so that you can add a new dimension to your cooking. Dry varieties such as fino and Pedro Ximenez work particularly well in this dish.

Sweet Sherry Onions with Morcilla

1 tablespoon butter

1 tablespoon extra virgin olive oil

1 bay leaf

300 g/11 oz baby onions, peeled

2 tablespoons fino (dry) or Pedro Ximenez sherry

1 tablespoon balsamic vinegar

1 tablespoon caster sugar

1 small bunch fresh flat-leafed parsley, finely chopped

200 g/7 oz morcilla (blood sausage) or mini cooking chorizo sausages

salt and freshly ground black pepper

Serves 4–6 as part of a selection of tapas

Heat the butter and olive oil in a large, non-stick frying pan until the butter has melted. Add the bay leaf and onions and cook for about 4–5 minutes, stirring regularly, until the onions are golden all over. Add the sherry, vinegar and sugar, reduce the heat and cook for a further 5–7 minutes, or until the onions are caramelised and soft. Remove from the heat, season to taste and stir in the parsley, then set aside while you prepare the morcilla.

If using large sausages, cut the morcilla or chorizo into about 1 cm/ ½ inch thick slices; keep mini sausages whole.

Heat a clean frying pan to medium hot, add the sausages and cook, turning frequently, until they are golden, cooked and the oils have run out – 5–7 minutes. Add the onions to the pan and cook together for a further 2–3 minutes. Serve warm.

Fish & Seafood

Serve these with good crusty bread – to me, the best part of eating mussels is soaking up the delicious juices. Saffron, the stigma of a species of crocus, is the most expensive spice in the world so I've made it optional, but do use it if you can as it gives a lovely colour.

I had a similar dish to this in one of my favourite restaurants in Auckland. There, the Asian-inspired mussels were baked with wasabi. My version uses garlic instead and is finished with a little chilli. Try to use New Zealand green-lipped mussels, which are larger than other ones.

Mussels in Wine, Tomato and Chilli Sauce

1 kg/2¼ lb mussels

2 tablespoons extra virgin olive oil

1 onion, peeled and finely chopped

½ teaspoon crushed chilli flakes

a pinch of saffron threads (optional)

2 tablespoons tomato paste

75 ml/3 fl oz red wine

a small handful of fresh flat-leafed parsley, chopped

salt and freshly ground black pepper

Wash the mussels thoroughly, remove the beards and discard any mussels that are broken or open.

Heat the olive oil in a large saucepan and sauté the onion for 2–3 minutes, or until soft and translucent but not browned. Add the chilli flakes, saffron and tomato paste and mix well. Add the red wine, then stir in the mussels, cover the pan and steam, shaking regularly, for 4–6 minutes, or until all the mussels are open. Discard any mussels that do not open. Stir in the parsley, season to taste and serve immediately.

Serves 4–6 as part of a selection of tapas

Alioli and Chilli-Grilled Mussels

12 cooked, green-lipped mussels, in the half shell

12 tablespoons Alioli (see page 19), or garlic mayonnaise

2 tablespoons smoked chilli jam, or sweet chilli sauce

Serves 4–6 as part of a selection of tapas

Preheat the grill to hot. Place the mussels in their half shell, flesh-side up, on a baking tray. Spread 1 tablespoon of alioli or mayonnaise over each mussel, to completely cover the flesh, then place ½ teaspoon of chilli jam or sweet chilli sauce on top.

Place under the grill and cook for 3–5 minutes, or until bubbling, slightly golden and each mussel is hot. Serve immediately with cocktail sticks.

If you have it available, use fresh white crab meat instead of tinned. However, tinned will also give you a very good result. The slightly spongy texture is typical of many fish balls I have tasted in Spain.

Crab and Lemon Balls

1 large egg, beaten

1 tablespoon fino (dry) sherry

a pinch of hot chilli powder

1 tablespoon mayonnaise

1 sprig fresh rosemary, finely chopped

zest of 1 lemon

170 g/6 oz tin white crab meat, drained

75 g/3 oz fresh breadcrumbs

about 1 tablespoon plain flour, for dusting

4 tablespoons extra virgin olive oil

salt and freshly ground black pepper

Serves 4–6 as part of a selection of tapas

Whisk the egg, sherry, chilli powder, mayonnaise, rosemary and lemon zest together in a bowl. Season well, then stir in the crab meat and breadcrumbs to form a firm but still wet mixture that can be shaped into balls. If the mixture is too wet, add more breadcrumbs.

Using dampened hands, shape the mixture into 12 heaped tablespoon-sized balls and place on a lightly floured plate. Chill, covered, for at least 30 minutes, or up to 12 hours.

Heat the olive oil in a large frying pan to medium heat. Add the crab balls and cook for 4–6 minutes, turning frequently to keep their round shape. The balls should be golden brown and cooked through.

Drain on kitchen paper and serve warm with cocktail sticks.

The Galician region in the northwest of Spain is famous for its shell-fish and locally produced cider. I've combined these two ingredients to make a true Galician delicacy. These are delicious with a salsa verde or Sweet Chilli and Red Pepper Salsa (see page 29) for dipping.

Scallop Fritters in Cider Batter

75 g/3 oz plain flour

1 egg, separated

1 tablespoon extra virgin olive oil

75 ml/3 fl oz cider at room temperature

1 litre/1¾ pints vegetable oil

300 g/11 oz scallops, halved if large

salt and freshly ground black pepper

lemon wedges, to serve

Serves 4 as part of a selection of tapas

Sift the flour into a medium-sized bowl and stir in ¼ teaspoon of salt. Make a well in the centre and set aside.

In a separate bowl, whisk the egg yolk, olive oil and cider together. Pour the liquid mixture into the flour well and stir, using a whisk, until just combined. Cover and refrigerate for 1 hour.

Whisk the egg white in a clean, grease-free bowl until stiff peaks form, then gently fold into the cider batter until just combined.

Heat the vegetable oil in a large, heavy-based saucepan to 190°C/375°F, or until a small cube of bread turns golden in about 30 seconds. If the scallops are large, remove the orange roes and cook them separately. Season the scallops (and roes) with salt and pepper.

When the oil is hot enough, using a spoon, dip the scallops into the batter, one at a time, and gently lower into the oil. Cook in batches for 1–2 minutes, or until golden brown and the scallop is cooked through.

Remove with a slotted spoon and drain on kitchen paper, then serve hot with lemon wedges on the side.

Best cooked on the barbecue and lightly charred on the outside, these little fish are good served with some crusty sourdough bread and a few grilled tomatoes for the ultimate in tapas combinations.

Many people think tinned whole tomatoes are inferior to fresh tomatoes, but they couldn't be more wrong. In fact, it is the best-quality tomatoes that are usually selected for the canning process, so they should be sweet, juicy and full of flavour.

Grilled Sardines

Clams in Cherry Tomato Sauce

12 small sardines

2 tablespoons lemon juice

2 tablespoons extra virgin olive oil

1 teaspoon dried crushed chillies

1 teaspoon dried oregano

sea salt

lemon wedges, to serve

Serves 4–6 as part of a selection of tapas

Make 2–3 shallow slashes on both sides of each sardine and set aside in a shallow dish.

Combine the lemon juice, olive oil, crushed chillies and oregano in a bowl and pour over the sardines. Leave to marinate for at least 30 minutes, or up to 12 hours.

Preheat a barbecue or griddle pan to hot and cook the sardines for 3–4 minutes on each side, or until opaque through and crispy on the outside. Serve sprinkled with sea salt, with lemon wedges on the side.

1 kg/2¼ lb clams, left to sit in cold, salted water for about 2 hours to expel any sand or grit

2 tablespoons extra virgin olive oil

1 small onion, peeled and finely chopped

1 fennel bulb, finely chopped

2 garlic cloves, peeled and chopped

2 tablespoons fino (dry) sherry

400 g/14 oz tin baby cherry tomatoes in juice

a small handful of torn fresh flat-leafed parsley

sea salt and freshly ground black pepper

Serves 4–6 as part of a selection of tapas

Wash the clams, discarding any that are cracked, broken or will not close.

Heat the olive oil in a large, heavy-based saucepan. Add the onion and fennel and cook slowly for 2–3 minutes until cooked but not browned.

Add the garlic, sherry, clams and tomatoes, with their juice, and stir, then cover the pan and cook the clams for a further 2–3 minutes, shaking the pan occasionally, or until most of the clams are open.

Stir in the parsley and season to taste, then turn out into a serving dish and discard any clams that have not opened.

Serve immediately with bread on the side to mop up any juices.

Pork goes particularly well with fish and shellfish and this dish is no exception. These tidy little skewers are the perfect tapa and are exceptionally good when cooked on the barbecue to give a slightly smoky and charred taste.

Fresh seafood with a squeeze of lemon juice is simplicity at its best. These not only taste good but they look great too.

Prawn and Chorizo Skewers

Barbecued Prawn and Scallop Skewers

12 raw king prawns, peeled (leave tails on if preferred) and deveined

1 tablespoon extra virgin olive oil

1 small bunch of fresh flat-leafed parsley, finely chopped

2 cooking chorizo sausages, about 150 g/5 oz each, cut into 1.5 cm/¾ inch thick slices

12 short bamboo skewers, soaked in water for as long as possible, up to 24 hours

Makes 12

Place the prawns in a bowl with the olive oil and parsley and mix to coat.

Place a slice of chorizo into the crook of each prawn and thread on to a skewer.

Cook the skewers on a preheated barbecue or under a hot grill for 5–7 minutes, turning once or twice, or until cooked and slightly charred. Serve immediately.

12 small scallops

4 spring onions, trimmed and each cut into three pieces, about 4 cm/ 1¾ inches long

12 raw king prawns, peeled (leave tails on) and deveined

extra virgin olive oil

sea salt and freshly ground black pepper

12 bamboo skewers, soaked in water for as long as possible, up to 24 hours

To serve

lemon wedges

Alioli (see page 19)

Makes 12

Using a small knife or your fingers, remove any membrane or hard white muscle from the scallops. Skewer one scallop on to each skewer, followed by a piece of spring onion. Curl up the prawns so that the ends meet and thread on to the skewer. Brush the skewers lightly with olive oil and sprinkle with a little salt and black pepper.

Cook the skewers on a preheated barbecue or under a hot grill for 1–2 minutes on each side, or until the seafood is just cooked. Serve hot with lemon wedges and alioli for dipping.

These little morsels melt in your mouth and give you a punch of heat afterwards. Perfectly accompanied by a cooling citrus yoghurt sauce, they go well with almost any selection of tapas and a chilled glass of white wine.

Blackened Salmon with Orange Yoghurt Sauce

300 g/10 oz salmon fillet, skinned and boned

2 tablespoons vegetable oil

1 teaspoon dried thyme

1 teaspoon dried rosemary

1 teaspoon dried oregano

½ teaspoon Spanish sweet smoked paprika

½ teaspoon cayenne pepper

1 garlic clove, peeled and crushed

1 teaspoon cumin seeds, lightly toasted

1 teaspoon fine salt

For the citrus yoghurt

300 ml/½ pint Greek yoghurt

zest and juice of 1 orange

60 ml/2fl oz extra virgin olive oil

Serves 4 as part of a selection of tapas

Cut the prepared salmon fillet into 2.5 cm/1 inch cubes. Coat the salmon in 1 tablespoon of the vegetable oil and then set aside in a large dish.

Combine the thyme, rosemary, oregano, paprika, cayenne, garlic, cumin seeds and salt in a small bowl. Generously coat the salmon cubes in the spice mixture and leave to sit while you prepare the yoghurt.

Put the yoghurt, orange zest and juice and the olive oil in a bowl and, using a small whisk, combine, then set aside.

Heat the remaining vegetable oil in a large, non-stick frying pan and cook the salmon for 3–4 minutes, turning frequently until golden all over and cooked through.

Serve warm with cocktail sticks and the yoghurt sauce for dipping.

The simplicity of this dish is what makes it so special. Crisp lettuce with salty anchovies, finished with nothing but the finest of extra virgin olive oils — what more could you want?

These really should come under the recipe for Banderillas (see page 20), but I thought they deserved recognition of their own. Sticky sweet onions wrapped in sharp anchovies are bliss.

Baby Gem Lettuce with Anchovies

Caramelised Onions Wrapped in Anchovies

2 baby gem lettuces

12 anchovies, tinned or marinated

extra virgin olive oil

freshly ground black pepper

Serves 4–6 as part of a selection of tapas

Remove and discard the outer leaves from the lettuce and chop the lettuce in half lengthways. Then chop each half into three lengthways wedges.

Place each wedge, pointy side up, on a serving plate and position 1 anchovy down its length. Drizzle generously with olive oil and season with black pepper.

1 quantity Sweet Sherry Onions (see page 67), omitting the morcilla or chorizo

about 18 anchovies marinated in vinegar and olive oil

Makes 18

Make the recipe for the onions and allow them to cool completely. (This recipe should give you about 18 baby onions.)

Wrap an anchovy around the circumference of each onion and secure it with a cocktail stick. Serve cold.

You will find a lot of deep-fried food in Spanish cooking and the use of oil is prolific. This is one dish you will see on the menu of almost every restaurant within a five-mile radius of the coast. Make sure you use very fresh squid and fry for only long enough to just cook it.

Deep-Fried Squid Rings

600 g/1 lb 5½ oz fresh squid

vegetable oil, for deep-frying

100 g/3½ oz plain flour, for coating

2 eggs, beaten with 1 tablespoon of water

100 g/3½ oz breadcrumbs

lemon wedges, to serve

Serves 4 as part of a selection of tapas

First prepare the squid. Pull out and discard the head and the attached intestines from the tube-like body and remove and discard the long, thin cartilage. Cut off the wings from the body and, using your fingers, pull the skin away and discard. Rinse the tubes under running cold water, then pat dry using kitchen paper. Cut the tubes into rings about 5 mm/ ¼ inch thick.

Heat the vegetable oil in a large, heavy-based saucepan to 190°C/375°F, or until a small cube of bread turns golden in about 30 seconds.

Put the flour, egg and breadcrumbs in three separate bowls and line them up in order. Dredge the squid rings in the flour, then dip them in the egg mixture and, finally, coat with the breadcrumbs. Deep-fry the squid for 1–1½ minutes, or until golden. Do not over-cook them or the squid will turn tough.

Remove with a slotted spoon and drain on kitchen paper, then serve immediately with lemon wedges on the side.

Ask your fishmonger for tenderised baby octopus, or you will have to go through the rigorous task of tenderising it yourself – this involves throwing it forcefully at a hard surface 30–40 times and is not a pleasant task.

If I put a plate of these in front of my partner, he'll devour them within minutes. I always serve them with crusty bread to mop up the lovely marinade. They are a useful standby to keep in the fridge and can be incorporated into many tapas, such as wrapped around baby onions.

Marinated Octopus and Fennel Salad

1.5 kg/3½ lb tenderised baby octopus

2 litres/3½ pints water

100 ml/3½ fl oz white wine vinegar

3 bay leaves

1 teaspoon black peppercorns

1 fennel bulb, shaved

75 ml/3 fl oz extra virgin olive oil

juice of 2 lemons

1 tablespoon chopped fresh dill

salt and freshly ground black pepper

lemon wedges, to serve (optional)

Serves 4–6 as part of a selection of tapas

Clean the octopus and remove and discard the head.

Pour the water into a large saucepan and bring to the boil. Add the vinegar, bay leaves, peppercorns and octopus and bring back to the boil, then boil for 20–25 minutes, or until the octopus is tender. (Test by cutting a bit off and tasting it.)

Remove the octopus from the saucepan and rinse it under running cold water, discarding any skin. Cut the octopus into bite-sized chunks and put into a large bowl. Add the fennel, olive oil, lemon juice and dill and mix well. Cover and leave to marinate overnight in the refrigerator.

Just before serving, season to taste and serve with lemon wedges, if liked.

Marinated Anchovies

100 g/3½ oz anchovy fillets, drained

1 small red onion, peeled and very finely chopped

1 small bunch of fresh flat-leafed parsley, roughly chopped

1 tablespoon capers, rinsed and roughly chopped

1 tablespoon red wine vinegar

4 tablespoons extra virgin olive oil

Serves 4–6 as part of a selection of tapas

Place the drained anchovies flat on a serving plate. Put the onion, parsley and capers in a small bowl, add the vinegar and olive oil and stir to combine.

Pour this marinade over the anchovies and leave to marinate for at least 30 minutes, or up to 48 hours.

I think fresh, succulent oysters are best eaten raw. However, if you prefer, just before serving you can put the dressed oysters under a preheated grill for 1–2 minutes. Cava is a sparkling Spanish white wine, but you can use any sparkling white wine if you can't find it.

Oysters with Cava Dressing

12 oysters, in their half shell

1 small red onion, peeled and very finely chopped

1 tablespoon sherry vinegar, or cider vinegar

50 ml/2 fl oz Cava, or other sparkling white wine

freshly ground black pepper

To serve

sourdough bread

lemon wedges

Makes 12 tapas-sized portions

Arrange the oysters in a single layer on a large serving platter. Place the onion, vinegar, Cava and black pepper in a small bowl and stir to combine.

Pour the dressing over the oysters and leave to marinate for up to 15 minutes before serving.

Serve with some sourdough bread, generously buttered, and some lemon wedges.

I ate these in Valencia under a laden orange tree. Even now, the smell of orange blossom takes me back to this one dish. The garlic chilli butter that remains after you've devoured all the prawns is great mopped up with some crusty bread.

There's nothing more satisfying than getting your fingers stuck into a bowl of whole barbecued prawns. Prepare a dipping bowl of water and lemon wedges so that people can wash their hands before moving on to the next tapas dish.

Baked Chilli-Butter Prawns

Garlic and Tio Pepe Prawns

2 tablespoons extra virgin olive oil

30 g/1 oz salted butter

1 large red chilli, deseeded and finely chopped

1 garlic clove, peeled and crushed

300 g/11 oz peeled and deveined raw king prawns

1 small bunch of fresh flat-leafed parsley, finely chopped

sea salt

Serves 4 as part of a selection of tapas

Preheat the oven to 180°C/350°F/mark 4. Heat the olive oil and butter in a small saucepan. Add the chopped chilli and garlic and sauté for 2–3 minutes until cooked but not browned.

Put the prawns in an ovenproof dish and pour over the butter mixture. Cook in the oven for 5–7 minutes, or until the prawns are cooked.

Remove from the oven, sprinkle over the parsley and sea salt and serve hot.

2 tablespoons extra virgin olive oil

2 garlic cloves, peeled and finely chopped

1 large red chilli, deseeded and finely chopped

2 kg/4½ lb raw unpeeled prawns

2 tablespoons Tio Pepe, or other dry sherry

a small handful of chopped fresh flat-leafed parsley

Serves 4 as part of a selection of tapas

Heat the olive oil in a large, non-stick frying pan. Add the garlic and chopped chilli and sauté quickly but do not brown.

Increase the heat, add the prawns and sherry and shake the pan over the heat until the prawns turn pink and are cooked – 2–3 minutes.

Remove from the heat, stir in the parsley and serve immediately.

Fresh squid quickly fried so that it melts in your mouth and served with garlic alioli is really a taste sensation that can't be surpassed.

Crispy Paprika-Salt Squid

400 g/14 oz prepared squid tubes

vegetable oil, for deep-frying

100 g/3½ oz plain flour

½ teaspoon Spanish hot smoked paprika

1 teaspoon salt

Alioli (see page 19)

Serves 4 as part of a selection of tapas

Rinse the squid under running cold water and pat dry using kitchen paper. Cut the tubes along one side to open them out. Using a sharp knife, lightly score the inside surface of each tube in a criss-cross pattern, making sure you do not cut right through. Then cut them into about 4 cm/1¾ inch pieces. Cut the tentacles, if you have them, into smaller bite-sized pieces.

Fill a heavy-based saucepan with vegetable oil and heat to 190°C/375°F, or until a small cube of bread turns golden in about 30 seconds.

While the oil is heating, combine the flour, paprika and salt in a bowl. Add the squid and mix until well coated. Shake off the squid and add to the oil in batches, cooking for 1–2 minutes each batch, or until golden, crispy and cooked through.

Remove with a slotted spoon and drain on kitchen paper. Serve warm with alioli on the side.

To me, stuffed baby squid is a true taste of the Mediterranean. I have taken on more of the flavours of North Africa for this particular dish, but a non-meat version using breadcrumbs, fresh herbs and lemon is a favourite, too. These are also delicious charred on the barbecue.

Stuffed Baby Squid

1 tablespoon extra virgin olive oil

1 small onion, peeled and very finely chopped

1 garlic clove, peeled and crushed

½ teaspoon cayenne pepper

½ teaspoon Spanish sweet smoked paprika

1 teaspoon ground cumin

1 tablespoon tomato paste

1 teaspoon caster sugar

200 g/7 oz pork mince

50 ml/2 fl oz white wine

1 tablespoon chopped fresh flat-leafed parsley

250 g/9 oz baby squid tubes, 5–6 cm/2–2½ inches long

plain flour, for coating

oil, for shallow-frying

sea salt and freshly ground black pepper

Makes about 18

Heat the olive oil in a large, non-stick frying pan. Add the onion, garlic, cayenne, paprika and cumin and sauté until the onion is soft and translucent but not browned. Stir through the tomato paste and sugar, then increase the heat and add the pork mince. Using a wooden spoon, break up the mince and cook for about 5 minutes. Add the wine, then reduce the heat and cook for a further 10–12 minutes. Stir in the parsley and season accordingly. Leave to cool.

To prepare the squid, trim off the wide end of each tube to neaten. Rinse the squid and pat dry, inside and out, using kitchen paper. Fill the tubes with the cooled mince mixture – but do not overfill – and secure the ends with cocktail sticks. Coat the squid in flour.

Heat the oil in a non-stick frying pan and, when hot, shallow-fry the squid for 2–3 minutes, or until the squid is just cooked. Sprinkle with sea salt and serve hot.

Salt cod is whole, gutted cod that has been coated with coarse sea salt and left to hang and dry, thus preserving it. Make sure you soak the salt cod for at least the time specified in order to de-salt it thoroughly. If you can, buy centre cuts of the fillet, which are the fatter and meatier ones. As an alternative, use 400 g/14 oz fresh cod fillets and season to taste.

Salt Cod Croquettes

400 g/14 oz salt cod, soaked in water for 24–36 hours and water changed 3–4 times

750 ml/1¼ pints milk

3 bay leaves

1 teaspoon black peppercorns

zest of 1 lemon, cut into large strips using a potato peeler

500 g/1 lb 2 oz floury potatoes, such as King Edward, peeled and cut into chunks

30 g/1 oz plain flour, plus extra for dusting

1 large bunch of fresh flat-leafed parsley or coriander, finely chopped

750 ml/1¼ pints vegetable or sunflower oil

freshly ground black pepper

To serve

lemon wedges

Alioli (see page 19)

Makes about 20

Drain the salt cod and place in a saucepan with the milk, bay leaves, peppercorns and lemon zest and bring to the boil. Reduce the heat and simmer for about 5 minutes, or until the fish flakes easily. Remove the salt cod from the milk and set aside to cool.

Pass the milk through a sieve and return the strained milk to the saucepan. Add the potatoes and bring to the boil, then reduce the heat and simmer for about 15 minutes, or until soft.

While the potatoes are cooking, pull the cod apart, discarding any bones or skin, and set aside in a bowl.

When the potatoes are cooked, drain and add to the cod along with the flour, parsley and a good grind of black pepper. Using a fork, mash all the ingredients together until well combined. Using a spoon and your hand, shape the mixture into croquettes, about 30 g/1 oz each, and set aside on a lightly floured tray or board.

Heat the vegetable or sunflower oil in a heavy-based saucepan to 190°C/375°F, or until a small cube of bread turns golden in about 30 seconds.

Cook the croquettes in batches for 2–3 minutes each batch, or until hot through and golden in colour.

Remove with a slotted spoon and drain on kitchen paper. Serve warm with lemon wedges and alioli on the side.

Whitebait from the UK and Mediterranean waters is different to the whitebait you will find in my homeland of New Zealand. If this large variety of whitebait is unavailable use whole anchovies or small sardines instead – just adjust the cooking time according to size.

This Galician speciality sauce is a favourite with poached fish. I like to use halibut, a firm white fish that holds its shape when poached. Monkfish works well, too, but you can choose a more flaky fish such as cod or haddock, if you prefer.

Fried Whitebait

Poached Halibut with Paprika Sauce

200 g/7 oz fresh whitebait

100 ml/3½ fl oz milk

plain flour, for coating

vegetable or sunflower oil, for deep-frying

sea salt

lemon wedges, to serve

Serves 4–6 as part of a selection of tapas

Dip the whitebait in the milk, then coat them in flour.

Heat the vegetable or sunflower oil in a large, heavy-based saucepan to 190°C/375°F, or until a small cube of bread turns golden in about 30 seconds.

Deep-fry the whitebait in the oil for 1–2 minutes, or until golden and crispy. Drain on kitchen paper and sprinkle with salt. Serve hot with lemon wedges on the side.

400 g/14 oz halibut fillets, cut into large chunky pieces

½ teaspoon black peppercorns

4 garlic cloves, peeled and cut into quarters

2 bay leaves

100 ml/3½ fl oz extra virgin olive oil

1–2 teaspoons Spanish hot or sweet smoked paprika

1 tablespoon white wine vinegar

4 tablespoons hot fish stock, or fish cooking liquid

Serves 4 as part of a selection of tapas

Put the halibut and peppercorns in a small frying pan or saucepan and just cover with boiling water. Bring to a gentle simmer and then simmer for 3–4 minutes, or until the fish is just cooked. Using a slotted spoon, remove from the liquid and transfer to several small serving dishes, or one large dish.

Put the garlic, the bay leaves and the olive oil in a saucepan and cook gently, without letting the garlic colour, until hot.

Remove from the heat and stir in the paprika, vinegar and hot fish stock or fish cooking liquid. Stir to combine, then pour the liquid evenly over the fish and serve immediately, garnished with the bay leaves from the sauce.

Cold fish – yuk! That's what I thought, too, when a similar dish was placed in front of me, but it's actually delicious. And the great thing is that it can be made in advance with no last-minute cooking. These fish medallions are incredibly fragrant and full of flavour and will simply melt in your mouth. The recipe does, however, require a firm fish that can withstand the long marinating.

Spanish Monkfish Medallions

For the marinade

4 tablespoons extra virgin olive oil

1 large onion, peeled and finely sliced

1 teaspoon cumin seeds

a large pinch of saffron threads

1 cinnamon stick, broken in half

1 garlic clove, peeled and crushed

1 sprig fresh thyme

zest and juice of 1 orange

50 ml/2 fl oz dry sherry

50 ml/2 fl oz cider vinegar

2 tablespoons runny honey

2 tablespoons extra virgin olive oil

600 g/1 lb 5½ oz monkfish fillets, cut into 2.5 cm/1 inch chunks

100 g/3½ oz seasoned plain flour

salt and freshly ground black pepper

Serves 6 as part of a selection of tapas

To make the marinade, heat the 4 tablespoons olive oil in a large, non-stick frying pan. Add the onion, cumin seeds, saffron and cinnamon stick and sauté for 3–4 minutes, or until the onion is softened but not browned. Add the garlic and thyme and sauté for a further 2–3 minutes. Add the orange zest and juice, sherry, vinegar and honey and bring to the boil. Boil for about 2 minutes, then remove from the heat, taste and season and transfer to a small bowl.

Wipe out the pan, add the 2 tablespoons olive oil and place over a medium heat. Coat the fish in the seasoned flour and cook in batches until golden and cooked through.

Transfer the fish to a serving plate and pour over the marinade. Leave to cool, then cover and refrigerate for up to 24 hours. Remove from the fridge 30 minutes before serving.

You can make these small, medium or large — whatever the occasion demands. As a tapa, they are best kept small so that you can pick them up and eat them in one mouthful. For a main meal, make four large fish cakes and serve with a green salad and lots of lemon wedges.

Salmon, Caper and Dill Fish Cakes

300 g/11 oz salmon fillet, skinned and boned

1 tablespoon extra virgin olive oil

1 small onion, peeled and very finely chopped

150 g/5 oz dry mashed potato

2 tablespoons capers, rinsed and roughly chopped

1½ tablespoons chopped dill

100 g/3½ oz plain flour, for coating

1 egg, beaten

about 100 g/3½ oz fresh breadcrumbs, for coating

about 30 g/1 oz butter

salt and freshly ground black pepper

lemon wedges, to serve

Serves 6 as part of a selection of tapas

Preheat the oven to 180°C/350°F/mark 4. Put the salmon on to an oiled baking tray and cook in the oven for 8–10 minutes, or until it is cooked and flakes when broken with a fork.

Heat the olive oil in a small saucepan and cook the onion for 3–4 minutes, or until softened but not browned.

Combine the mashed potato, onion and flaked salmon in a large bowl and, using a fork, mix well. Stir in the capers and dill. Taste and season accordingly. Refrigerate the mixture for at least 1 hour.

Put the flour, egg and breadcrumbs in three separate bowls and line them up in that order. Roll the mixture into tablespoon-sized balls and flatten with the palm of your hand. Coat each fish cake in the flour, then dip in the beaten egg and, finally, roll each in the breadcrumbs to coat.

Heat half the butter in a large frying pan and cook half the fish cakes for 2–3 minutes on each side, or until hot through and golden brown. Repeat with the remaining butter and fish cakes.

Serve hot or warm with lemon wedges.

This Catalonian speciality uses ingredients such as almonds and saffron which were brought to Spain by the Moors as early as the 7th century. Almond trees now grow prolifically in the area. The sauce is basically a romesco sauce without peppers and with saffron added.

White Fish in an Almond, Saffron and Bread Sauce

4 tablespoons extra virgin olive oil

50 g/2 oz blanched almonds

2 garlic cloves, peeled and sliced

2 slices of fresh thick white bread, crusts removed and roughly torn

50 ml/2 fl oz fino (dry) sherry

a pinch of saffron threads

1 onion, peeled and finely chopped

1 large beef tomato, finely diced

150 ml/¼ pint boiling water

500 g/1 lb 2 oz skinless cod, monkfish or other firm white fish, cut into about 20 cubes

salt and freshly ground black pepper

fresh flat-leafed parsley, to serve (optional)

Serves 4 as part of a selection of tapas

Heat 3 tablespoons of the olive oil in a large, non-stick frying pan and fry the almonds for 2–3 minutes. Add the garlic and bread and continue frying until they are lightly golden and most of the oil has been absorbed. This will only take a few more minutes.

Remove from the heat and place in a food processor with the sherry and saffron, then whiz to a paste.

Cook the onion in the remaining oil for 3–4 minutes, or until translucent but not browned. Stir in the almond mixture, tomato and boiling water and simmer for about 3 minutes. Season the sauce to your liking, then add the fish, cover and cook for a further 3–5 minutes, stirring once, or until the fish is just cooked.

Serve hot, sprinkled with flat-leafed parsley, if liked.

Ask your fishmonger to fillet the sardines – if you're not a dab hand with the filleting knife, it can be a fiddly job. You need to start preparing these at least three days before you want to eat them.

Marinated Sardines with Shaved Fennel

100 g/3½ oz sea salt

8 large sardines, filleted

125 ml/4 fl oz cider vinegar

500 ml/17 fl oz water

3 bay leaves

1 onion, peeled and chopped into chunks

1 fennel bulb, cut into chunks

½ teaspoon black peppercorns

125 ml/4 fl oz extra virgin olive oil

To serve

1 fennel bulb, very finely shaved or sliced

salt and freshly ground black pepper

Serves 4 as part of a selection of tapas

Sprinkle half the sea salt into a large, non-metallic dish (glass or plastic is best) and place the filleted sardines on top. Sprinkle over the remaining salt, cover and refrigerate for about 24 hours.

Put all the remaining ingredients, except the olive oil, into a saucepan and bring to the boil, then reduce the heat and simmer for 30 minutes. Take off the heat and leave to cool completely.

When the sardines have had 24 hours in salt, wipe off the salt and put them back into a clean, non-metallic dish. Pour over the cooled vinegar liquid and refrigerate for a further 24 hours.

Remove the sardines from the vinegar and again place in a clean, non-metallic dish. Cover with the olive oil and refrigerate for at least 24 hours, or up to 1 week.

Serve the marinated sardines topped with very finely shaved or sliced fennel and seasoned with salt and black pepper.

These succulent, juicy fritters are simple to make. Chickpea flour, also known as gram flour, has an unmistakable yellow colour and a matte finish. It has a dry, earthy aroma and slightly nutty taste. If you can't find it, substitute potato or rice flour, or just use all plain flour.

Prawn Fritters

½–1 teaspoon chilli powder

100 g/3½ oz chickpea flour, or gram flour

60 g/2½ oz plain flour

a generous pinch of salt

about 200 ml/7 fl oz cold water

400 g/13 oz raw, peeled prawns, roughly chopped

1 garlic clove, peeled and crushed

a small handful of fresh flat-leafed parsley, chopped

olive oil, for frying

lemon wedges, to serve

Makes 15

Put the chilli powder, chickpea or gram flour, the plain flour and salt in a large bowl. Slowly add the water, using just enough to make a pouring batter, ensuring that all the flour is mixed in.

Gently stir in the prawns, garlic and parsley.

Heat about 1 tablespoon of olive oil in a large, non-stick frying pan. Fry large spoonfuls of the prawn batter in batches until cooked and golden brown on both sides – 3–4 minutes. Replenish the oil as necessary between batches Drain on kitchen paper.

Serve warm with lemon wedges on the side.

Vegetables & Salads

Piquillo peppers (also called pimiento) are peppers that have been cooked and peeled and are ready-prepared to be used in dishes. They are widely available these days and should easily be found at your supermarket in either tins or jars.

Depending on the time of year, these can be served hot or cold. Either way they are delicious, and they also work well as a party canapé. For a completely vegetarian option, make the olive paste without anchovies.

Walnut and Cheese-Stuffed Piquillos

Cherry Tomatoes Stuffed with Olive Paste

100 g/3½ oz fresh walnuts, roughly chopped

75 g/3 oz soft goat's cheese

2 tablespoons chopped soft herbs, such as parsley, tarragon, chives

zest of 1 small lemon

150 g/5 oz tin small piquillo peppers (about 12 in a tin)

freshly ground black pepper

Makes about 12

Combine the walnuts, goat's cheese, herbs and lemon zest in a bowl, then season with black pepper.

Place the peppers on a flat surface and spoon a heaped teaspoonful of the mixture into each one. Transfer to a serving plate and chill.

Serve cold.

12 cherry tomatoes

4 tablespoons Black Olive Paste (see page 15)

extra virgin olive oil

flat-leafed parsley, to serve

Makes 24

If you are serving these warm, preheat the oven to 180°C/350°F/mark 4. Halve the cherry tomatoes crossways and, using a teaspoon, carefully scoop out the pulp and discard it.

Place the tomato halves, cut-side up, on a baking tray, or on a serving dish. Spoon ½ teaspoon of olive paste into each tomato half and drizzle with olive oil. If serving warm, bake in the oven for 5–7 minutes, or until hot through and the tomato is cooked but not yet collapsing. Remove from the oven.

Garnish each tomato half with a sprig of parsley and a good grind of black pepper, then serve.

These can easily become a vegetarian tapa by taking out the prosciutto (ham). Adjust the seasoning accordingly and hey presto!

Stuffed Mushrooms

1 tablespoon extra virgin olive oil, plus extra for greasing

250 g/9 oz (about 12) closed cup mushrooms, chestnut or white, stems removed and set aside

2 shallots, peeled and finely chopped

1 garlic clove, peeled and chopped

1 teaspoon finely chopped rosemary

3 slices of Serrano ham or prosciutto, finely sliced

50 g/2 oz goat's cheese

4 tablespoons fresh breadcrumbs

salt and freshly ground black pepper

Serves 4–6 as part of a selection of tapas

Preheat the oven to 190°C/375°F/mark 5. Lightly grease a baking tray. Wipe the mushrooms with a damp paper towel to remove any dirt. Roughly chop the mushroom stems and set aside.

Heat the olive oil in a large, non-stick frying pan and sauté the shallots for 2–3 minutes, or until soft and translucent but not browned. Add the garlic, rosemary, mushroom stems and black pepper to taste and sauté for a couple of minutes. Add the ham and stir to combine.

Remove from the heat and transfer to a bowl. Stir in the goat's cheese and breadcrumbs and season to taste. Place 1 heaped teaspoon of the mixture into each mushroom and place on the baking tray.

Bake for 8–10 minutes, or until lightly golden and the mushrooms are cooked. Serve hot.

Nothing is more thirst-quenching on a hot summer's afternoon than a small cup of gazpacho on ice; alternatively, you can heat it up for a winter warmer. Gazpacho was originally made by field workers, who combined their oil and bread rations with water and salt and added whatever vegetables they had available – namely tomatoes and peppers – to produce a thick vegetable soup.

Gazpacho

about 60 g/2½ oz stale white bread

1 small red onion, peeled and chopped

½ cucumber (200 g/7 oz) peeled and deseeded

600 g/1 lb 5½ oz (about 6) tomatoes, skinned and deseeded

1 red pepper, deseeded and chopped

2 garlic cloves, peeled and finely chopped

1 teaspoon toasted cumin seeds

½–1 teaspoon Spanish hot smoked paprika, to taste

1 tablespoon extra virgin olive oil

2 tablespoons sherry vinegar or red wine vinegar

a pinch of sugar (optional, depending on the sweetness of your tomatoes)

50 ml/2 fl oz ice-cold water

salt and freshly ground black pepper

Serves 6

Put the bread in a shallow dish, cover with water and leave to soak for 10–15 minutes, but no longer.

Put the onion in a separate bowl, cover with boiling water and leave to soak for the same time. Drain the onion.

Put the bread, onion, cucumber, tomatoes, chopped pepper, garlic, cumin seeds, paprika and olive oil in a food processor. Whiz well, then add the vinegar, sugar, if needed, and the water. Push the soup through a fine sieve, adding a little extra chilled water if it is too thick. Season to taste, cover and chill until needed.

To serve, pour into small glasses or bowls, over ice if liked.

Not typically Spanish, but these little tartlets show the benefit of seasonal cooking. For more rustic and hearty tartlets, choose a selection of wild mushrooms in autumn.

Mixed Mushroom and Aubergine Tartlets

1 large aubergine

20 ml/¾ fl oz extra virgin olive oil

375 g/13 oz puff pastry

50 g/2 oz soft goat's cheese

300 g/11 oz mixed mushrooms, such as porcini, girolles, button, chopped into small chunks or slices

a good splash (about 2 tbsp) of any type of Madeira or sherry

a small handful of fresh flat-leafed parsley, chopped

salt and freshly ground black pepper

Makes 12–16

Preheat the oven to 200°C/400°F/mark 6. Put the aubergine on a baking tray, brush with about 1 teaspoon of the olive oil and bake for 25–30 minutes, or until soft and cooked. Remove from the oven and leave to cool slightly.

While the aubergine is cooling, cut the puff pastry into 12–16 rounds about 7 cm/3 inches in diameter. Place on a baking tray and impress a second round into each, about 6 cm/2½ inches in diameter, ensuring that you do not cut right through. Bake in the oven for 8–12 minutes, or until golden and puffed.

When they are cooked, remove from the oven and, using a small knife, cut around the inner circle and remove the disc of pastry. This can be used as a top if liked, or pushed down into the case.

Now, peel the aubergine and mix with the goat's cheese, then season to taste and set aside.

Heat the remaining olive oil in a large frying pan and sauté the mushrooms until golden brown. While the pan is still hot, add the Madeira or sherry and let it evaporate. Stir through the parsley and season well.

Put a spoonful of aubergine mixture and a heaped pile of mushrooms into each pastry case and serve warm or cool.

If you are on a wheat-free diet, these tarts are a treat. The heart of the artichoke is scooped out and shaped into a 'tart' case, which is then filled with this delicious pancetta mixture. They can easily be made into a vegetarian's dream, too, by leaving out the pancetta.

Artichoke, Pea and Pancetta Tarts

6 large globe artichokes

juice of 1 lemon

250 ml/8 fl oz white wine

250 ml/8 fl oz passata (tomato pulp)

2 sprigs fresh rosemary

2 tablespoons extra virgin olive oil

100 g/3½ oz peas, fresh or frozen

2 shallots or baby onions, peeled and finely chopped

150 g/5 oz cubed pancetta

1 egg, beaten

1 tablespoon milk

75 g/3 oz goat's cheese

Makes 6

Firstly, prepare the artichokes. Using a sharp knife, slice each stem off at the base and snap away the leaves one by one and discard them. Trim the base of any dark green bits and use a small spoon to dig out the furry choke. Rub the artichokes immediately with lemon juice and put the bases into a small saucepan.

Add the wine, passata, 1 rosemary sprig and 1 tablespoon of olive oil to the pan. Bring to the boil, then reduce the heat and simmer for 20–25 minutes, or until the bases are tender. Leave to cool in the liquid.

When you are ready to cook them, preheat the oven to 200°C/400°F/ mark 6. Bring a small saucepan of water to the boil and blanch the peas for 2–3 minutes, or until just cooked. Cool them under running cold water and set aside.

Heat the remaining oil in a large, non-stick frying pan. Finely chop the remaining rosemary sprig, then add to the pan with the chopped onion and pancetta and sauté until golden. Remove from the heat and stir in the peas.

To assemble the tartlets, remove the artichoke bases from the liquid and pat dry. Place them flat on a baking tray and spoon the pancetta mixture into them. Combine the beaten egg and milk and spoon over the tartlets, then crumble over the goat's cheese.

Bake in the oven for 10–15 minutes, or until the filling is set and lightly golden.

Serve warm or cold, either whole or cut into quarters.

A springtime treat that is delicious served with a platter of cold meats. Try adding some fresh peas or broad beans to the omelette for an extra dose of greens.

Asparagus Omelette

250 g/9 oz asparagus, trimmed

1 tablespoon extra virgin olive oil

1 onion, peeled and finely chopped

1 garlic clove, peeled and crushed

50 g/2 oz finely grated Parmesan or Manchego cheese

6 large eggs, beaten

salt and freshly ground black pepper

Makes 12 tapas-sized portions

Cut the asparagus into 2.5 cm/1 inch pieces and blanch in boiling water for 3–4 minutes, then drain. Run the pieces under cold water until cool, then set aside.

Heat the olive oil to medium in a 30 cm/12 inch non-stick fry pan. Sauté the onion for 2–3 minutes, or until softened and cooked but not browned. Add the garlic and asparagus and sauté for a further minute, then stir in the cheese and season generously with salt and black pepper. Pour in the beaten eggs and shake the pan so that everything is evenly distributed, but do not stir. Reduce the heat, cover the pan and leave to cook for 8–10 minutes, or until the egg is set.

Remove from the heat and serve warm or cold, cut into small wedges or squares.

This recipe uses floury potatoes, which have a low moisture content and are higher in starch than waxy potatoes. They may start to disintegrate slightly while you're frying them, but this just adds to the texture of the tortilla. In some parts of Spain they make their tortilla completely with mashed potato, so this is somewhat of a compromise.

Spanish Tortilla (Tortilla Española)

75 ml/3 fl oz extra virgin olive oil

about 6 medium (1 kg/2¼ lb) floury potatoes, such as King Edward or Russet, peeled, quartered and thinly sliced (2–3 mm/⅛ inch thick)

1 medium onion, peeled and thinly sliced

6 large eggs

salt

Makes 12 tapas-sized portions

Heat the olive oil in a 25–30 cm/10–12 inch non-stick frying pan. Sauté the sliced potatoes and onion, lifting and turning them until cooked but not brown – this will take 15–20 minutes.

Beat the eggs together in a large mixing bowl and season well with salt. When the potatoes are cooked, using a slotted spoon, transfer them into the egg mixture, leaving as much oil behind as possible. Strain the oil from the pan and reserve.

Heat 1 tablespoon of the reserved oil in the same pan over a medium heat. Add the egg and potato mixture, spreading the potatoes evenly in the pan. Cook the tortilla, covered, for 5–6 minutes, gently shaking the pan so that it doesn't stick.

Slide a long spatula underneath the tortilla, then place a large plate over it and quickly turn it over on to the plate. Add another tablespoon of oil to the pan and quickly slide the tortilla back in. Tuck the sides in with a fork and cook for a further 3–4 minutes, or until it is firm and set.

Remove the tortilla from the pan and leave to cool to room temperature before serving, cut into wedges.

Grated carrots don't always need to remind you of your childhood. Try this salad, which with the addition of haloumi and harissa is a grown-up's dream!

Carrot, Haloumi and Harissa Salad

500 g/1 lb 2 oz (about 3 large) carrots, peeled

1 small bunch of fresh flat-leafed parsley, roughly chopped

2 tablespoons extra virgin olive oil

250 g/9 oz haloumi cheese, cut into 1 cm/½ inch cubes

For the marinade

4 tablespoons extra virgin olive oil

1 teaspoon caraway seeds

1 teaspoon cumin seeds

1 garlic clove, peeled and crushed

2 teaspoons harissa paste

2 tablespoons red wine vinegar

1 teaspoon caster sugar

Serves 4–6 as part of a selection of tapas

Grate the carrots into a large bowl, then set aside while you prepare the marinade.

Heat the olive oil in a small saucepan or frying pan and add the caraway and cumin seeds, the garlic and harissa paste. Cook for 1–2 minutes, or until aromatic and the garlic turns golden in colour. Remove from the heat and stir in the vinegar and sugar. Pour over the carrots, mix well and set aside in the fridge to marinate for at least 1 hour, or up to 24 hours.

Just before serving, remove the carrot from the fridge to bring it back to room temperature and stir in the parsley. Heat the olive oil in a frying pan to medium hot, then add the haloumi cubes and fry for 3–5 minutes, or until golden brown. Remove from the heat and drain on kitchen paper. Allow to cool slightly, then mix into the carrot.

You'll find this dish throughout Spain in many different shapes and forms. Really, it's just fried potatoes in a spicy tomato sauce. Sometimes peppers might be added to the sauce, or the potatoes may be thinly sliced and fried rather than cut into chunks.

Spicy Fried Potatoes (Patatas Bravas)

4 tablespoons extra virgin olive oil

6 medium (about 1 kg/2¼ lb) floury potatoes, such as King Edward, peeled and cut into 4 cm/ 1¾ inch cubes

1 large onion, peeled and finely chopped

2 garlic cloves, peeled and finely chopped

2 red chillies, deseeded and finely chopped, or ½–1 teaspoon dried crushed chillies

½ teaspoon ground cumin

2 tablespoons red wine vinegar

400 ml/14 oz tin chopped tomatoes

1 teaspoon caster sugar

salt

Serves 4–6 as part of a selection of tapas

Preheat the oven to 220°C/425°F/mark 7. Heat 3 tablespoons of the olive oil in a large, non-stick frying pan until hot. Add the potatoes and sauté until golden brown all over. Transfer the potatoes and any remaining oil to a baking dish and cook in the oven until the potatoes are crisp – about 15 minutes.

While the potatoes are cooking, prepare the sauce. Heat the remaining olive oil in a frying pan over a medium heat. Sauté the onion for 2–3 minutes, or until cooked and translucent but not browned.

Add the garlic, chillies and cumin and sauté for a further 2 minutes. Add the remaining ingredients and simmer the sauce for a further 10–12 minutes.

Drain the potatoes from the oil (if there is any remaining) and place in one large or several small serving dishes. Pour over the sauce and serve hot.

Waxy potatoes have a high moisture content and are low in starch. They will tend to hold their shape a lot better than floury potatoes and are ideal in salads, or in recipes such as this where potatoes are boiled or roasted.

The red paprika oils will leech out from the sausages, giving this salad a fiery tinge. I like to use 'picante', or 'hot', sausages, but it's up to you.

Saffron Potatoes, Egg and Watercress

6 medium (about 1 kg/2¼ lb) waxy potatoes, such as Roseval, Desiree or Pink Fir Apple

4 tablespoons extra virgin olive oil

50 g/2 oz butter

a large pinch of saffron threads

4–6 eggs, boiled for 5 minutes, then plunged into cold water and peeled

1 bunch of watercress, washed and trimmed to remove any coarse stalks

Alioli (see page 19), to serve (optional)

sea salt and freshly ground pepper

Serves 4–6 as part of a selection of tapas

Boil the potatoes in their skins until cooked but still firm – 10–12 minutes. Allow to cool slightly, then peel and cut each into 8–10 wedges.

Heat the olive oil and butter in a large, non-stick frying pan until the butter starts to foam. Add the saffron and potatoes and cook until the potatoes are tender and golden in colour. Season generously with salt and black pepper, then put the potatoes on one large or several small plates.

Cut the eggs in half lengthways and place on top of the potatoes, yolk-side up. Scatter over the watercress and serve with a generous dollop of alioli.

Chickpea and Chorizo Salad

½ tablespoon extra virgin olive oil

2 (about 200 g/7 oz) cooking chorizo sausages, sliced lengthways then into 1 cm/½ inch pieces

1 red pepper, deseeded and diced into 1 cm/ ½ inch cubes

2 tablespoons dry Madeira, or red wine

400 g/14 oz tin chickpeas, drained and rinsed

3 spring onions, trimmed and finely sliced

fine salt and freshly ground black pepper

Serves 4–6 as part of a selection of tapas

Heat the olive oil in a large, non-stick frying pan and cook the chorizo and diced pepper for 3–4 minutes.

Add the Madeira and sauté for a further 30 seconds, then add the chickpeas and cook until the chickpeas are hot and the chorizo is thoroughly cooked.

Remove from the heat and stir in the spring onions and seasoning to taste. Serve warm with crusty bread.

This is basically a Catalan version of roasted vegetables. Slow-cooked and delicious, they are also a perfect accompaniment to meat or fish dishes.

Escalivada

2 red peppers

1 medium aubergine

2 small red onions

4 tomatoes

3 garlic cloves, unpeeled

3–4 tablespoons extra virgin olive oil

juice of 1 lemon

salt and freshly ground black pepper

Serves 4–6 as part of a selection of tapas

Preheat the oven to 200°C/400°F/mark 6. Wash all the vegetables well and dry them using kitchen paper. Lay them in a single layer with the garlic on a large baking tray and add just enough olive oil to lightly coat them – 2–3 tablespoons. Season with salt and black pepper.

Roast in the oven for 20–25 minutes, or until they are soft but still holding their shape and the skins are loosened and slightly charred in parts. Remove from the oven and leave to cool.

When the vegetables are cool, peel off all the skins and chop the vegetables into large chunks. Squeeze the garlic from their skins. Arrange on a platter, or in small tapas dishes.

Combine the lemon juice and remaining olive oil in a separate bowl and season well. Pour over the vegetables and serve warm or cold.

Spanish Rice Balls with Melting Manchego Centres

These deep-fried rice croquettes are more popular in the north than in the south of Spain. There they use the short-grained paella rice that is prolific in the plains of Catalonia. These rice balls must be eaten warm so that the cheesy Manchego centre oozes as you bite into it.

Spanish Rice Balls with Melting Manchego Centres

1 tablespoon extra virgin olive oil

15 g/½ oz butter

1 onion, peeled and finely diced

a pinch of saffron threads

a pinch of turmeric

1 garlic clove, peeled and crushed

300 g/11 oz Spanish paella rice

750 ml/1¼ pints hot vegetable stock

150 g/5 oz frozen or fresh peas

1 litre/1¾ pints sunflower or vegetable oil

2 eggs, lightly beaten

100 g/3½ oz Manchego cheese, cut into 1 cm/ ½ inch cubes

100 g/3½ oz dried breadcrumbs

salt and freshly ground black pepper

Heat the olive oil and butter in a large, non-stick frying pan. Add the onion and sauté for 2–3 minutes, or until translucent but not browned. Stir in the saffron, turmeric and garlic and sauté for a further minute. Add the rice and stir through until slightly translucent around the edges.

Pour in all the hot stock and bring to the boil. Reduce the heat to a simmer and leave to simmer for 20–25 minutes, adding the peas after 15 minutes and stirring occasionally, or until the rice is cooked and the liquid is absorbed. Season well, tasting as you do so, and set aside to cool completely.

Pour the sunflower or vegetable oil into a large, heavy-based saucepan and put over a low heat while you prepare the rice balls.

Add the beaten eggs to the cooled rice mixture and stir well to combine. Take golf ball-sized amounts of the mixture and shape into rounds. Press a piece of cheese into the centre of each round and shape the ball around it. Roll each ball in breadcrumbs and set aside on a lightly crumbed board.

The oil is hot enough when a small cube of bread dropped into it turns golden in about 30 seconds. Place 4–5 balls into the oil at a time and cook for 3–4 minutes, or until they are evenly golden. Remove each batch with a slotted spoon and drain on kitchen paper while you cook the rest. They can be kept warm in a low oven as you go.

Serve warm so that the cheese centre oozes out.

Makes 36–40

If you're having trouble with your pan and the tortilla seems to be sticking – don't panic! Don't attempt to flip it, but instead heat up the grill and finish cooking the top of the tortilla under the grill. Once the tortilla is cooked and cooled slightly, use a long spatula to loosen the bottom and you should be able to flip the tortilla straight out on to a plate.

Red and Green Pepper Tortilla

150 ml/5 fl oz extra virgin olive oil

about 4 medium (600 g/1 lb 5½ oz) floury potatoes, such as King Edward or Russet, peeled, quartered and thinly sliced (2–3 mm/ ⅛ inch thick)

1 medium onion, peeled and thinly sliced

1 red pepper, deseeded and thinly sliced

1 green pepper, deseeded and thinly sliced

6 large eggs

salt

Makes 12 tapas-sized portions

Heat the olive oil in a 25–30 cm/10–12 inch non-stick frying pan. Sauté the sliced potatoes, onion and peppers, lifting and turning them until cooked but not brown – this will take 15–20 minutes.

Beat the eggs together in a large mixing bowl and season well with salt. When the potatoes are cooked, using a slotted spoon, transfer them into the egg mixture, leaving as much oil behind as possible. Strain the oil from the pan and reserve.

Heat 1 tablespoon of the reserved oil in the same pan over a medium heat. Add the egg and potato mixture, spreading the potatoes evenly in the pan. Cook the tortilla, uncovered, for 5–6 minutes, gently shaking the pan so that it doesn't stick.

Slide a long spatula underneath the tortilla, then place a large plate over it and quickly turn it over on to the plate. Add another tablespoon of oil to the pan and quickly slide the tortilla back in. Tuck the sides in with a fork and cook for a further 3–4 minutes, or until firm and set.

Remove the tortilla from the pan and leave to cool to room temperature before serving, cut into wedges.

I prefer these served as a cold dish, since the flavour seems to develop more and more. If you're trying to impress, keep the little green ends on the carrots and add a touch of honey for sweetness.

You don't need to stick strictly to the vegetables listed below – for a change, try using cauliflower, pumpkin or asparagus. If you don't want to make up any of the suggested accompaniments below, a bought sweet chilli sauce also goes well, or a squeeze of lime juice.

Paprika and Cumin-Spiced Carrots

300 g/11 oz baby carrots, trimmed (see above)

1 teaspoon cumin seeds

1 tablespoon sesame seeds

1 teaspoon ground coriander

1 teaspoon Spanish hot smoked paprika

½ teaspoon fine salt

1 teaspoon caster sugar

2 tablespoons extra virgin olive oil

1 tablespoon red wine vinegar

1 small bunch of fresh flat-leafed parsley, finely chopped

Serves 4–6 as part of a selection of tapas

Cook the carrots in boiling water for 3–4 minutes, or until cooked but still firm to the bite, or al dente. Rinse them under cold running water and set aside.

Toast the cumin and sesame seeds in a dry, heavy-based saucepan until fragrant and golden. Remove from the heat and stir in the ground coriander, paprika, salt, sugar, olive oil, vinegar and parsley.

Stir this mixture into the warm carrots and serve immediately, or set aside to cool.

Battered Vegetables

150 g/5 oz plain flour, plus extra for coating

50 g/2 oz cornflour

250 ml/8 fl oz cold water

a pinch of salt

½ teaspoon white wine vinegar

1 large egg yolk

1 large courgette, thinly sliced on the diagonal

1 aubergine, thinly sliced crossways

1 red pepper, deseeded and cut lengthways into 1.5 cm/¾-inch wide strips

1 onion, peeled and thickly sliced

750 ml–1 litre/ 1¼–1¾ pints vegetable or sunflower oil

Sweet Chilli and Red Pepper Salsa or Alioli, to serve (see pages 29, 19)

Serves 4–6 as part of a selection of tapas

Put the flour and cornflour in a large mixing bowl. Slowly whisk in the water to form a smooth paste. Add the salt, vinegar and egg yolk and mix well. Refrigerate the batter for at least 15 minutes, or up to 1 hour.

Prepare the vegetables and set aside. Heat the oil in a heavy-based saucepan to 190°C/375°F, or until a small cube of bread turns golden in about 30 seconds. Dip the vegetables in flour, then in the batter and deep-fry in batches for 3–4 minutes, or until golden and cooked.

Remove with a slotted spoon and drain on kitchen paper. Serve immediately with Sweet Chilli and Red Pepper Salsa or Alioli for dipping.

The colour, flavour and aroma of honey depend on the flower that the nectar has been taken from. Orange blossom honey brings the Spanish element to this dish, but choose whatever flavour you like best, from the subtle to the more fragrant.

Fried Goat's Cheese Balls with Honey

75 g/3 oz plain flour

1 egg, lightly beaten

75 g/3 oz breadcrumbs

12 balls (about 200 g/7 oz) goat's cheese, drained, or a 200 g/7 oz chunk, cut into 2.5 cm/ 1 inch cubes

750 ml/1¼ pints vegetable or sunflower oil

2–3 tablespoons runny honey

Makes about 12

Put the flour, egg and breadcrumbs in three separate bowls and line them up in order. Dust the goat's cheese balls in the flour, dip them in the beaten egg, then roll them in the breadcrumbs. Set aside and refrigerate until you are ready to cook.

Heat the vegetable or sunflower oil in a large, heavy-based saucepan to 190ºC/375ºF, or until a small cube of bread turns golden in about 30 seconds. Cook the balls for 3–4 minutes, or until golden brown and the cheese is oozing in the centre. Remove with a slotted spoon and drain on kitchen paper.

Transfer to a serving plate, drizzle over the honey and serve immediately with cocktail sticks.

This salad is refreshing on the palate and cleansing to the liver.
For a more dramatic look, use blood oranges when they're in season.
I sometimes like to add a tin of white tuna in oil for a slightly more
substantial tapa.

Valencia Orange, Fennel and Black Olive Salad

3 Valencia oranges, or other juicy oranges such as blood or navel

1 fennel bulb

75–100 g/3–3½ oz black olives

3 tablespoons extra virgin olive oil

juice of 1 lemon

freshly ground black pepper

a small handful of fresh flat-leafed parsley, to serve

Serves 4–6 as part of a selection of tapas

Peel the oranges, removing all the white pith, then finely slice. Using a mandoline or very sharp knife, finely shave the fennel into thin slices. Combine the oranges, fennel and olives in a large bowl.

In a separate bowl, combine the olive oil, lemon juice and black pepper. Pour this dressing over the salad, gently combine and leave to marinate in the fridge for at least 1 hour, or up to 12 hours.

Just before serving, scatter over the parsley leaves and serve cold.

If you're serving them hard-boiled, regular eggs would work just as well in this recipe. Use 4–6 and, once cooked, cut them into quarters lengthways.

Quail Eggs with Paprika Sesame Salt

24 quail eggs

For the spice mix

1 tablespoon coriander seeds

1 tablespoon cumin seeds

2 tablespoons white sesame seeds

2 tablespoons sea salt flakes

1 teaspoon freshly ground black pepper

½ teaspoon Spanish hot smoked paprika

Makes 24

Put the quail eggs in a pan and cover with cold water. Bring to the boil and cook for 2½ minutes for soft-boiled, or 3½ minutes for hard-boiled. Drain the eggs and cool them under running cold water. Reserve a few eggs in their shells for garnish and peel the remainder, then set aside.

Heat a heavy-based frying pan to medium heat and add the coriander, cumin and sesame seeds and the salt. Stir continuously for 2–3 minutes, or until the seeds are aromatic and slightly golden. Transfer to a mortar and, using a pestle, roughly crush the seeds but do not grind to a fine powder. Stir in the black pepper and paprika, then put the spice mix in a small dish.

Put the peeled eggs in a bowl, garnish with the whole eggs and serve with the spice mix for dipping.

Sherry is a wine full of intense depth and complex flavours. Produced in Jerez, in southern Spain, it has a rich history and has always been an essential part of Spanish cuisine. It comes in many different styles, from pale golden and dry to the dark and rich with a soft sweet finish.

This goat's cheese and pepper combo is a match made in heaven. The sweet, succulent peppers can be topped with a small cube of quince paste, but it's optional. If you are stuck for time, just buy a jar of piquillo peppers (see page 102) and use them in the same way.

Mushrooms with Garlic and Sherry

3 tablespoons extra virgin olive oil

50 g/2 oz butter

4–6 garlic cloves, peeled and sliced

a pinch of Spanish hot smoked paprika

500 g/1 lb 2 oz button mushrooms, sliced into 5 mm/ ¼ inch thick slices

salt

3 tablespoons dry or sweet sherry

1 tablespoon fresh flat-leafed parsley, roughly chopped

Serves 4–6 as part of a selection of tapas

Heat the olive oil and butter in a large, non-stick frying pan to medium hot. Add the garlic and paprika and sauté briefly but do not brown.

Increase the heat and add the mushrooms, then sauté, stirring constantly, until golden and the oil has been absorbed. Season with salt. Add the sherry and simmer briefly so that the flavour can be absorbed.

Remove from the heat, sprinkle over the parsley and serve immediately.

Trio of Roasted Peppers with Goat's Cheese

3 peppers, preferably 1 each of red, yellow and orange, or a mix

1 tablespoon extra virgin olive oil, plus extra to serve

1 tablespoon runny honey

2 large sprigs fresh thyme

100 g/3½ oz goat's cheese, cut into twelve chunks

75–100 g/3–3½ oz Quince Paste (Membrillo, see page 30), cut into small cubes (optional)

sea salt and freshly ground black pepper

Makes 12 tapas-sized portions

Preheat the oven to 180°C/350°F/mark 4. Cut each pepper in half, deseed and remove the core, then halve again. Place the peppers, cut-side up, in a single layer on a baking tray. Drizzle the olive oil and honey over the peppers, then roughly tear over the thyme sprigs and season generously with salt and black pepper.

Roast in the oven for 18–20 minutes, or until cooked and slightly charred around the edges. Remove from the oven and leave to cool for 20–30 minutes.

When the peppers are cool enough to handle, place a cube of goat's cheese and quince paste, if using, in the centre of each. Roll up and secure with a cocktail stick. Serve warm, drizzled with some olive oil.

Roasting asparagus really intensifies its flavour. Sprinkled with sea salt and some of your finest extra virgin olive oil, the stems are perfect as they are, but sometimes we want something just a little bit more special and that's why I've included my recipe for tarragon salsa verde.

White asparagus is cut while it is below the ground – the lack of light prevents the production of chlorophyll and the asparagus from turning green. Fresh white asparagus must be peeled up to the tip to remove the tough outer skin, and needs longer cooking than green asparagus.

Roasted Asparagus with Salsa Verde

White Asparagus with Dipping Sauces

500 g/1 lb 2 oz asparagus, trimmed

1 tablespoon extra virgin olive oil

sea salt and freshly ground black pepper

For the salsa verde

1 small red onion, peeled and very finely diced

1 garlic clove, peeled and crushed

2 tinned anchovies in oil, drained and finely chopped

1 tablespoon capers, roughly chopped

½ teaspoon Dijon mustard

1 tablespoon cider vinegar

15 g/½ oz tarragon, finely chopped

15 g/½ oz fresh flat-leafed parsley, finely chopped

about 4 tablespoons extra virgin olive oil

Serves 4–6 as part of a selection of tapas

Preheat the oven to 180°C/350°F/mark 4. Place the asparagus in a single layer on a baking tray with shallow sides. Sprinkle generously with salt and pepper and drizzle over the olive oil. Roast in the oven for 10–12 minutes (depending on the thickness of the asparagus), or until tender to the bite and cooked through.

While the asparagus are cooking, combine all the ingredients for the salsa verde in a bowl and mix well, adding extra olive oil if liked. Season to taste.

Serve the asparagus warm with the salsa verde drizzled over, or as a dipping sauce.

1 bunch of fresh white asparagus, or 350 g/12 oz jar (about 8–12 stems) white asparagus

1 tablespoon extra virgin olive oil

100 ml/3½ fl oz Alioli (see page 19)

1 tablespoon chopped fresh dill

100 ml/3½ fl oz Romesco Sauce (see page 15)

Serves 4–6 as part of a selection of tapas

If using fresh asparagus, peel the stems and drop them into cold water.

Heat 1 tablespoon olive oil in a frying pan. Add the asparagus and turn to coat them in the oil, stirring continuously so that they don't colour, then add about 250 ml/8 fl oz of water. Cover and leave to simmer for 3–4 minutes, then remove the lid and simmer until the water has evaporated and the asparagus are cooked. If using cooked asparagus in a jar, drain and place on a serving platter.

Combine the alioli and dill in a small bowl and mix well. Put the herbed alioli and the romesco sauce in two separate serving bowls and place on the same platter as the asparagus. To eat, dip the asparagus in the sauces.

These small pies are popular in Spain. This vegetarian version is baked, rather than deep-fried, as is normal. The rich buttery pastry wrapped around salty olives and cheese melts-in-your-mouth when served warm. These are delicious served with an ice-cold glass of fino sherry.

Cheese and Olive Empanadas

1 quantity Empanada Pastry (see page 31), or 500 g/1 lb 2 oz bought puff pastry

200 g/7 oz soft goat's or sheep's cheese

1 egg, lightly beaten

100 g/3½ oz pitted green olives, roughly chopped

plain flour, for dusting

30 g/1 oz butter, melted

freshly ground black pepper

Makes 24–30

Prepare the pastry and refrigerate until ready to assemble the pies. Preheat the oven to 200°C/400°F/mark 6.

Put the cheese, egg and chopped olives in a bowl and mix well, then season with black pepper.

Roll the pastry out on a lightly floured surface to approximately 3–4 mm/¼ inch thick and, using a 9–10 cm/3¾–4 inch round cutter, cut out circles.

Place a heaped teaspoon of the filling on one half of each round of pastry. Dip your finger in water and slightly dampen the pastry edges (to help them stick), then fold the pastry over the filling to make a half-moon shape. To seal the empanadas, pinch the edges of the pastry firmly together, then press down on the edges with the prongs of a fork to finish.

Brush the empanadas with melted butter and bake in the oven for 15–18 minutes, or until golden and puffed. Serve hot or warm.

Manchego is a sheep's cheese and varies from mild and quite soft to strong and hard. I like to choose the more mature and intensely flavoured variety for this tapas dish. The cheese melts and becomes oozy, so they must be eaten quickly while still hot.

Deep-Fried Manchego Cubes with Membrillo

100 g/3½ oz plain flour

1 egg, lightly beaten

100 g/3½ oz dried breadcrumbs

200 g/7 oz Manchego cheese, cut into 2.5 cm/1 inch cubes

750 ml–1 litre/1¼–1¾ pints vegetable or sunflower oil

100 g/3½ oz Quince Paste (Membrillo, see page 30), cut into 1 cm/½ inch cubes

Makes 20

Put the flour, egg and breadcrumbs in three separate bowls and line them up in order. Coat the cheese cubes heavily in the flour, dip them in the beaten egg, then roll them in the breadcrumbs. Set aside on a lightly floured board.

Heat the vegetable or sunflower oil in a large saucepan to 190°C/375°F, or until a small cube of bread turns golden in about 30 seconds. Cook the cheese cubes for 1–2 minutes, or until golden brown – the cheese inside should be soft and melted. Remove with a slotted spoon and drain on kitchen paper.

Place a cube of membrillo on top of each cheese cube and secure with a cocktail stick. Transfer to a serving plate and serve immediately while still warm and oozy.

Serve the following as part of a selection of tapas: throw them together into a salad and drizzle with extra virgin olive oil, or serve alongside toasted breads or crostini as toppings.

Roasted Garlic

1 large, unpeeled garlic bulb

extra virgin olive oil

Preheat the oven to 150°C/300°F/mark 2. Rub the whole garlic bulb lightly with oil, place in a roasting dish and cover the dish with foil.

Roast in the oven for 1–1½ hours depending on the size of the garlic, until it is very soft and tender. (Older garlic may take longer, so don't rush it.)

Allow to cool, then squeeze the flesh out of each clove.

Roasted Peppers

a selection of peppers – red, yellow, orange and green, washed and dried

Preheat the oven to 200°C/400°F/mark 6. Place the peppers on a large roasting tray and roast for 25–30 minutes, or until softened and slightly charred.

Allow to cool completely, then cut each in half, deseed and peel.

Roasted Aubergines

Roasted Cherry Tomatoes

1 large aubergine

extra virgin olive oil

Preheat the oven to 200°C/400°F/mark 6. Lightly rub the aubergine with a little olive oil and place on a baking tray. Roast in the oven for 25–30 minutes, or until soft and slightly charred.

Allow to cool completely, then peel.

2–3 bunches cherry tomatoes on the vine

1–1½ tablespoons extra virgin olive oil, plus extra to serve

sea salt and freshly ground black pepper

Preheat the oven to 200°C/400°F/mark 6. Put the tomatoes on a baking tray and drizzle over the olive oil. Season generously, then roast for 15–20 minutes, or until cooked and the juices are starting to ooze.

Serve warm or cold as a garnish, or on their own, drizzled with some of the finest extra virgin olive oil.

Haloumi is both salty in taste and squeaky in texture, with a firmness that holds its shape when cooked. It has an almost meaty substance, so it can be a good alternative for vegetarians. Dress it like you would a salad, and serve with a few salad leaves on the side – delicious.

Grilled Haloumi with Herbs

300 g/11 oz haloumi cheese, cut into 8–10 slices about 1 cm/ ½ inch thick

1½ tablespoons extra virgin olive oil, plus extra to serve

For the dressing

4 tablespoons extra virgin olive oil

juice and zest of 1 lemon

½ teaspoon Spanish sweet smoked paprika

2 tablespoons chopped fresh herbs, such as parsley, coriander, chives, mint

freshly ground black pepper

Serves 4 as part of a selection of tapas

Preheat a griddle pan to very hot. Rub the haloumi slices lightly with olive oil and grill them for 2–3 minutes on each side, or until grill marks form and the cheese is warmed through.

Combine all the dressing ingredients in a small bowl. Pour some dressing over the hot haloumi and serve immediately, or leave to cool. You can serve the extra dressing on the side for people to add to taste.

This hearty gratin is best made in small tapas dishes and served with several forks so that everyone can dig in. They can be prepared in advance up to the last stage. Just bake them off, or reheat them in the oven when needed so that they are steaming hot and golden brown.

Aubergine, Manchego and Piquillo Pepper Gratin

2 large aubergines, about 600 g/1 lb 5½ oz total weight

olive oil, for brushing

30 g/1 oz butter

2 tablespoons plain flour

600 ml/1 pint cold milk

75 g/3 oz finely grated Manchego cheese

1 egg, lightly beaten

250 g/9 oz piquillo peppers (see page 102)

salt and freshly ground black pepper

Makes 6 small or 1 large tapas

Preheat the grill to very hot and preheat the oven to 200°C/400°F/mark 6. Cut the aubergines into 1 cm/½ inch thick slices and brush with olive oil. Chargrill the aubergine for 2–3 minutes on one side and about 2 minutes on the other side, or until cooked and soft. Set aside while you make the sauce.

Melt the butter in a heavy-based saucepan. Stir in the flour and cook, stirring, until it turns yellow – this means the roux is cooked. Stir in the milk, little by little to avoid lumps, and continue stirring until the mixture thickens. It should be thick enough to coat the back of a spoon. Remove from the heat and stir in two-thirds of the cheese. Season to taste and leave to cool slightly, then stir in the beaten egg.

Use six individual tapas plates or ramekins, or one larger ovenproof dish. Layer the aubergine, sauce and peppers alternately into the plates, ramekins, or dish, finishing with the peppers. Sprinkle over the remaining cheese and a good grind of black pepper. Bake in the oven for 15–20 minutes, or until bubbling and golden. Serve hot or warm.

Manchego (sheep's cheese) and membrillo (quince paste) is an inspired union of flavours. Produced in the region of La Mancha, Manchego is one of Spain's iconic symbols and can now be found in many supermarkets worldwide.

Manchego with Membrillo (Quince Paste)

100 g/3½ oz wedge Manchego cheese, at room temperature

100 g/3½ oz Quince Paste (Membrillo, see page 30), or bought membrillo

Makes 6 tapas-sized portions

Trim the rind from the cheese and cut into six wedges. Place the cheese in a single layer on individual plates, or on one large plate.

Slice the quince paste into six pieces and place one slice on top of each wedge of cheese. Serve.

After sampling this tapa in a bar in the heart of Valencia, my friend Sara and I thought it impossible to bring this salad to life. The key is to not overcook the vegetables, use fresh not frozen, and don't drown it in mayo. Probably not traditional at all now, but much more tasty!

Russian Salad

100 g/3½ oz new potatoes

50 g/2 oz freshly shelled peas

100 g/3½ oz white tinned tuna in olive oil (preferably Ortiz brand)

1 hard-boiled egg, roughly chopped

2 tablespoons mayonnaise

1 tablespoon chopped fresh chives, plus extra to garnish

a pinch of Spanish sweet smoked paprika

1 chicory, separated into leaves

salt and freshly ground black pepper

Serves 4–6 as part of a selection of tapas

Boil the potatoes for 8–10 minutes, or until cooked but still firm. Run them under cold water and leave to cool, then cut into cubes about 1 cm/½ inch.

Cook the peas in boiling water for 2–3 minutes, or until just cooked. Cool completely under running cold water.

Combine all the ingredients, except the chicory, in a bowl and season to taste. Set aside until you are ready to serve.

Separate the chicory into individual leaves, wash and carefully dry, using kitchen paper. Place the leaves on a plate, cup-side up. Spoon the salad mixture into the chicory leaves and serve garnished with extra chives.

Index